"In a brilliant and profound analysis of Mary She~~~~~ ~~~~~~ the crucial moral question of where the seemingly insane pace of our technological powers to dominate nature is taking us, while ethical concerns of our responsibility to life and to nature are increasingly side-lined and ignored. He contrasts the utilitarian 'spectator mind' of Victor Frankenstein with the aesthetic sensibilities of the Monster he has created who awakens to the beauty and marvel of nature with wonder and awe, thereby drawing the comparison between the detached 'objective' approach of the scientist and the aesthetic sensibility of the poet's sense of relationship with the life around him. He raises the immensely important question of whether, in having the power to do something with our technological mastery, we should proceed to do it. He asks us to awaken from our current Frankensteinian dream of dominating nature and exploiting her resources for our own ends in time to prevent us destroying the unique and beautiful planet we inhabit."

—**Anne Baring, PhD, Jungian analyst and author of** *The Dream of the Cosmos: A Quest for the Soul*

"Professor Romanyshyn has brought to bear his unique blend of scholarship and creative reverie on this novel by Mary Shelley. First discussed in an earlier book thirty years ago, that early meditation on Shelley's *Frankenstein* has matured and born fruit. This wonderful collection of related essays are a culmination of decades of genuine thinking by one of psychology's most renowned writers. It is, of course, ultimately a book about us, mirrored in that two-hundred-year-old dream."

—**Roger Brooke, PhD, Professor of Psychology, Duquesne University, USA**

"In this deeply reflective work, Romanyshyn turns his gaze upon Shelley's creation and awakens us to the monsters we have crafted through our technological hubris: Monsters that haunt us daily manifesting in the likes of global environmental destruction. Read this work and come to know monsters both inner and outer."

—**Jeffrey T. Kiehl, Jungian analyst, author of** *Facing Climate Change*

"In this important, innovative and imaginative work, Robert Romanyshyn dreams the dream of Mary Shelley's classic novel *Frankenstein* onward and serves as a doctor for Dr. Frankenstein's monstrous shadow, the shadow of our unconscious technological civilization. With a phenomenological, poetic and Jungian archetypal sensibility, Romanyshyn raises fundamental questions, which unveil the hubris and unbridled inflations that have led to disastrous consequences for our time. Looking directly into the darkest recesses of our personal and cultural depths, he courageously calls us to a new vision and to an ethical and aesthetic renewal of our relationship to nature and the divine."

—**Stan Marlan, PhD, ABPP, author of** *The Black Sun: Alchemy and the Art of Darkness*

"As a young woman, Mary Shelley wrote a story that has universal appeal and mythic power. Robert Romanyshyn helps us apply that powerful vision in our day by offering penetrating questions and a broad scope. I found the writing beautiful and the analysis eye-opening. With help from this enlightening book, Frankenstein still speaks to you and me with humanistic hope."

—**Thomas Moore, author of *Care of the Soul***

"In today's world, science is offering us an array of utopian visions of humanity that is able to survive without human bodies, to replace plant and animal food sources with genetically modified versions, to design perfect babies and to colonize space. Mary Shelley's *Frankenstein*, created two centuries ago, struggled with similar questions in regard to the role of technology, ethics and relationships. *Victor Frankenstein, the Monster and the Shadows of Technology: The Frankenstein Prophecies* invites us into a dialogue about these important questions in regard to the contemporary world through evoking not only our historical and social awareness but our own imagination and our very human longings to conquer ourselves and our world, and by doing that to create and to face the Monster(s)."

—**Oksana Yakushko, PhD, Chair, Clinical Psychology Program, Pacifica Graduate Institute, USA**

"C. G. Jung argued that visionary works of art are prophetic, a notion that literary studies also generated in its own way. Although this is a uniquely multidisciplinary work of Jungian arts-based research, *Victor Frankenstein, the Monster and the Shadows of Technology: The Frankenstein Prophecies* by Robert Romanyshyn contributes to rapidly expanding debates in psychology, ecology, philosophy and literary studies. As a radical, intimate, poetic critique of a canonical novel that is central to literary degrees, this book is critical for reading Shelley's novel as prophetic of climate change, of the crisis in psyche and technology, as anticipating philosophies of the nonhuman, and, above all in this anxiety-ridden twenty-first century, for finding hope!"

—**Susan Rowland, PhD, author of *Remembering Dionysus***

"This long awaited book from Robert Romanyshyn on Mary Shelley's *Frankenstein* draws deeply on the story of the Creature who longs for relationship with his creator, who sees him only as a devil, unworthy of even a name. Romanyshyn weaves a tender teaching around eight questions when Victor's Monster, who haunts the margins of his maker's work, summons us out of the light. His work is an invitation to listen in the frailty of darkness and he shows us how attending to the Monster might transform us sufficiently to give hospitality to what has been exiled and silenced, for want of a name. He not only attends to the untold tale told by the Monster, which carries the prophetic shadow of his maker's dream to become a new god of creation, he also uncovers seeds of hope that are buried in Mary Shelley's story. It is a beautiful book so responsive to many of the crises we face today and I warmly welcome it."

—**Mary Smail, HCPC, UKCP, founder of SoulWorks UK—*telling the untold story***

VICTOR FRANKENSTEIN, THE MONSTER AND THE SHADOWS OF TECHNOLOGY

The Frankenstein Prophecies

Robert D. Romanyshyn

Routledge
Taylor & Francis Group

LONDON AND NEW YORK

First published 2019
by Routledge
2 Park Square, Milton Park, Abingdon, Oxon OX14 4RN

and by Routledge
52 Vanderbilt Avenue, New York, NY 10017

Routledge is an imprint of the Taylor & Francis Group, an informa business

© 2019 Robert D. Romanyshyn

British Library Cataloguing in Publication Data
A catalogue record for this book is available from the British Library

Library of Congress Cataloging-in-Publication Data
Names: Romanyshyn, Robert D. (Robert Donald), 1942- author.
Title: Victor Frankenstein, the monster and the shadows of technology : the Frankenstein prophecies / Robert D. Romanyshyn.
Description: Abingdon, Oxon ; New York, NY : Routledge, 2019. |
Includes bibliographical references and index.
Identifiers: LCCN 2018059980 (print) | LCCN 2019006143 (ebook) |
ISBN 9780429028335 (Master eBook) | ISBN 9780429650451 (Adobe Reader) |
ISBN 9780429645174 (Mobipocket) | ISBN 9780429647819 (ePub) |
ISBN 9780367137311 | ISBN 9780367137311q(hardback) |
ISBN 9780367137328(paperback) | ISBN 9780429028335(ebk)
Subjects: LCSH: Shelley, Mary Wollstonecraft, 1797-1851. Frankenstein. |
Jung, C. G. (Carl Gustav), 1875-1961. | Literature and technology. |
Psychoanalysis and literature.
Classification: LCC PR5397.F73 (ebook) | LCC PR5397.F73 R66 2019 (print) |
DDC 823/.7--dc23
LC record available at https://lccn.loc.gov/2018059980

ISBN: 978-0-367-13731-1 (hbk)
ISBN: 978-0-367-13732-8 (pbk)
ISBN: 978-0-429-02833-5 (ebk)

Typeset in Bembo
by Taylor & Francis Books
Printed by CPI Group (UK) Ltd, Croydon CR0 4YY

VICTOR FRANKENSTEIN, THE MONSTER AND THE SHADOWS OF TECHNOLOGY

In *Victor Frankenstein, the Monster and the Shadows of Technology: The Frankenstein Prohecies*, Romanyshyn asks eight questions that uncover how Mary Shelley's classic work *Frankenstein* haunts our world. Providing a uniquely interdisciplinary assessment, Romanyshyn combines Jungian theory, literary criticism and mythology to explore answers to the query at the heart of this book: who is the monster?

In the first six questions, Romanyshyn explores how Victor's story and the Monster's tale linger today as the dark side of Frankenstein's quest to create a new species that would bless him as its creator. Victor and the Monster are present in the guises of climate crises, the genocides of our "god wars," the swelling worldwide population of refugees, the loss of place in digital space, the Western obsession with eternal youth and the eclipse of the biological body in genetic and computer technologies that are redefining what it means to be human. In the book's final two questions, Romanyshyn uncovers some seeds of hope in Mary Shelley's work and explores how the Monster's tale reframes her story as a love story.

This important book will be essential reading for academics and students of Jungian and post-Jungian theory, literature, philosophy and psychology, psychotherapists in practice and in training, and for all who are concerned with the political, social and cultural crises we face today.

Robert D. Romanyshyn is Emeritus Professor of Psychology at Pacifica Graduate Institute, an affiliate member of the Inter-Regional Society of Jungian Analysts, and a Fellow of the Dallas Institute of Humanities and Culture, USA.

To those who have been exiled to the margins,
whose voices have been silenced,
whose stories are still un-told.

CONTENTS

ACKNOWLEDGMENTS

Although my name is on the cover of this book, I am after all only the author and who writes the book is a community of companions living and dead who carry the unfinished business of this shadow work, which attends to what lingers on and haunts the margins of our technological world.

Therefore, with gratitude for their support and company along the way, a nod of recognition and a silent whisper of thanks to the invisible ones who waited for me each morning to continue this work.

To my contemporaries special thanks are to be given to Veronica Goodchild. She sees the darkness in the light and the light in the darkness and her joyous presence has been a continuous inspiration along the many paths into the shadows. Her comments on the early versions of my manuscript were crucial to its final shape. Without her steadfast belief in the importance of making a place for the Monster to tell his side of Mary Shelley's story this book would not be.

Anne Baring also deserves special thanks. In a crucial moment when I felt I could not continue she warned me about the dangers of abandoning this work. In addition, I thank her for her careful reading of my manuscript and her valuable suggestions.

Special thanks too are due to Mary Smail. A master of movement, she and her students embodied and animated the key figures of the story in the London workshops we did together. In those presentations ideas took on shape and form.

I also wish to acknowledge the many colleagues whose encouragement for this book has been indispensible and whose work has informed my own reflections. I especially want to acknowledge Michael Sipiora for our many inspiring, challenging and insightful philosophical discussions over the many years of our friendship, Susan Rowland who has taught me to appreciate the literary side of Jung's psychology, Glen Slater for his thought provoking essays on cyborg culture, Dennis Slattery for his portrayal of Victor Frankenstein in the one time stage performance of a part of this work, Stan Marlan, my long time friend whose generosity toward my work over the years has been a sustaining influence, Thomas Moore who encouraged me to write this work for a wider audience, and Jeff Kiehl for our on going conversations about dreams and climate change.

Finally a word of thanks to Robyn Cass whose cheerful and optimistic presence shouldered the burdens of securing permissions for this book.

INTRODUCTION

According to Mary Shelley, *Frankenstein; Or, The Modern Prometheus* was born from a waking dream. Her dream has fascinated us for 200 years. But, as her story has foreseen some of the dire consequences of the high-tech world we are creating at an exhilarating but insane pace, her dream is now alarming us.

In her commentary on Mary Shelley's story, Joyce Carol Oates says, "The monsters we create by way of an advanced technological civilization 'are' ourselves as we cannot hope to see ourselves—incomplete, blind, blighted, and, most of all, self-destructive. For it is the forbidden wish for death that dominates." In this context, she adds that *Frankenstein* "is a parable for our time, an enduring prophecy, a remarkably acute diagnosis of the lethal nature of denial: denial of responsibility for one's actions" (Oates, 1984, pp. 249, 252).

Victor Frankenstein, the Monster and the Shadows of Technology: The Frankenstein Prophecies makes a place for the Monster to tell his side of the story. Created and abandoned by his maker, he carries the nightmare side of that dream that darkens Frankenstein's noble but flawed wish to be a new god who would banish death from the human condition. Attending to his tale, we have a chance to see more clearly how our unbridled enthusiasm for technological innovations and our denial of responsibility for their potential consequences have created monstrous problems.[1]

In Mary Shelley's story, Frankenstein personifies the exciting, developing scientific spirit of his times in the guise of a modern Prometheus, the titan who stole fire from the gods for the benefit of humanity. The Monster's tortured presence in the story, his violence and the trail of destruction and death that he leaves in his wake, remind us that the gods punished Prometheus for his hubris, for violating the boundary between the divine and the human orders.

Have the gods of old become our monsters?

When we act as if we are gods do we create monsters?

And, when we do, then, like Frankenstein, have we not faced the consequences by avoiding the question "Who is the Monster?"[2]

Questions play a large role in the format of *The Frankenstein Prophecies*. Indeed, they shape the style of the book as a series of essays, as attempts at reading Mary Shelley's story from the Monster's point of view, assaying the more or less untold tale that lies on the margins of her story. Questions open moments to pause and reflect on what otherwise might be unnoticed and unacknowledged. They are in fact intended to distract us as readers from what we have believed her story to be, to disturb our fixed images of Victor Frankenstein and the Monster. Open to the questions, readers might also find themselves, as I have as the writer, being questioned in ways that unsettle fundamental assumptions about the unexamined use of our powers of science and technology.[3]

In *The Frankenstein Prophecies* we meet Victor Frankenstein and his Monster as they have escaped the borders of the book and have become deeply embedded within the cultural imagination. In Questions One through Six we explore the ways in which Victor Frankenstein's Promethean hubris, his materialistic and utilitarian attitudes toward nature and the human body, and his contrast between himself as a man of science and his beloved wife to be, Elizabeth Lavenza, who, as a fragile and delicate creature busies herself with the airy creations of the poets, appear today in the guise of six contemporary crises. From climate crises with their destructive impact on nature to the terrorism of the "god wars" among our major religions, the swelling worldwide population of refugees, and the ways in which our genetic and computer technologies are redefining what it means to be a human being without a body, Victor Frankenstein's story and the Monster's tale continue to haunt us.

In Questions Seven and Eight, *The Frankenstein Prophecies* explores some seeds of hope that are also present in Mary Shelley's story. Who is the Monster?, the theme of Question Seven, nurtures the seed of a radical ethics that stands as a counterpoint to the lethal nature of denial that characterizes Victor Frankenstein. Other seeds of hope explored in Question Eight discuss Mary Shelley's story as a love story when and if love is not corrupted by blind power, as a tale that recovers our aesthetic ties to nature, and as a story that recovers the value and wisdom of the dream as a balancing check on the hubris of acting as if we are the new gods of creation.

Notes

1 Throughout this book I will use capital letters for the word Monster to underscore two key points: First, Monster emphasizes that he, as well as his maker, Victor Frankenstein, have escaped the borders of the book and now live on in the cultural imagination and indeed haunt us with their vivid presence; Second, Monster also points to his autonomy. It is a name, or at least a place-holder until we come to know his name, which differentiates Victor's use of the adjective monster, along with devil and demon, to further disown him and thus deny his own responsibility for his actions.

2 These three questions are dramatically portrayed in Guillermo del Toro's film *The Shape of Water* (Dale & del Toro, 2017), for which del Toro won a Golden Globe award for best director and the film the Oscar as best film: First, the so called monster is actually a

creature from the waters of the Amazon where it (he) is revered as a god and indeed in several scenes in the film the so called monster displays remarkable curative god like powers; second, when captured by an employee of the US military the creature is seen as a monster and treated cruelly—the intention is to exploit whatever value he might have as a potential military asset; third, the relationship that forms between the so called monster and the young woman who is without a voice increasingly raises the question for the audience of who in fact is the monster. Moreover, their relation includes her co-worker who is a black woman and her neighbor who is something of a failed artist. All three who befriend the monster are marginal figures for the scientific and military group that exploits the creature. In the final scenes of the film it is the character who has captured the creature for the military who says of the monster with an astonished sense of realization, "he is a god." In that moment the monster becomes the mirror that reflects the face of the character who exploited him for the military.

3   In an earlier version of this book I amplified the importance of questions by differentiating among three kinds of questions in the following ways: There were those questions that arose in my reading of Mary Shelley's story. They were embedded within the text of this book and on occasion were placed on a separate line for emphasis.

There were also questions that came to me as I was writing this book. Following clues dropped by the Monster, repeating with me a pattern he used with his maker Victor Frankenstein to draw him toward a final meeting where he hoped to be witnessed and heard by his maker, those questions slowed me down. They were indented one space and were in italic type; finally, there were those questions that had done more than slow me down. They stopped me in my tracks and even turned me upside down. They were the Monster's questions, whispered on the margins. They were also indented one space but were in bold type.

While I abandoned this process because, as two readers of my manuscript said, it interrupted the narrative flow and dramatic tone of the book, this difference among the three kinds of questions is discussed in Question Seven. In addition, with the format of questions that I have adopted, many of the questions are elaborated with scholarly material that draws on psychological, literary, philosophical and historical amplifications. These amplifications, which are now in the notes for each question, provide context for and are markers where the story of Mary Shelley and the Monster's untold tale might move forward. I encourage readers to linger with them along the way, as one might with a companion on a journey.

Question One

RESURRECTING THE DEAD

Is Mary Shelley's story a prophecy of the dangers of acting as gods?

The trauma of his mother's death is the event that sets Victor Frankenstein on his path to banish death from life. Death is now the ultimate Other, the "Spoiler" as he calls it, and, thankful that he has escaped the clutches of this Spoiler, he commits himself to the work of learning the secrets of life so that he might reverse the spoils of death.[1]

Frogs' legs and hanged criminals

Victor's opposition to death leads him into his experiments with reanimating dead tissue through the use of electrical stimulation. A severed leg of a frog, for example, would contract when a current was passed through it, suggesting that electricity was the vital spark of life. The process, accidently discovered in the late eighteenth century by Luigi Galvani, became widespread in the nineteenth century. In fact, Mary Shelley's husband, Percy Shelley, was attracted to the science and even experimented with it. These experiments were a source of amazement and entertainment for audiences who would gather around to witness what seemed like a miracle. The fascination with its possibilities was such that in 1803 Giovanni Aldini, the nephew of Galvani, progressed from frog legs to applying the process to the body of a hanged criminal, George Foster, who had murdered his wife and child. Those who witnessed the event claimed that when the current was passed through his body, one of Foster's eyes opened, his right hand was raised and his legs twitched.

Born within Mary Shelley's dream, Victor Frankenstein is conceived in the ambience of these discoveries at a time when distinctions are being made between absolute and apparent death and when the boundaries between life and death are vague and being debated. The internet of its day, the *Encyclopedie*, the most comprehensive collection of knowledge at the time and edited between 1751 and 1772 by Denis Diderot and Jean le Rond d'Alembert, even went so far as to declare

"That there is no remedy for death is an axiom widely admitted; we, however, are willing to affirm that death can be cured" (Arasse, 1991, p. 37).

Imagine that—death can be cured!

Beneath such a claim is the fantasy of immortality, which is the cry of the broken heart in young Victor Frankenstein's dream to overcome death. It is a fantasy that lives on today in the questions of what define death and when human life begins. Is one dead when the heart stops beating, or is brain death the measure? Does human life begin in the first contact of sperm and egg, or not until sometime after that moment? The latter is a question that not only drives the abortion debate, but also ties both questions to the controversies concerning the boundaries between science and religion.

On each side of this divide there is also a fundamental difference between life and death as matters of fact and matters of value. Victor's dream begins on the side of life as a value, which when someone dies wounds the heart. But he quickly leaps beyond that loss, and life and death become, as he declares, merely ideal boundaries that can be breached. And breach them he does, resolutely proceeding from frog legs to reanimating dead tissue to ultimately resurrecting the dead.

"I succeeded in discovering the cause of generation and life; nay, more, I became myself capable of bestowing animation upon lifeless matter" (Shelley, 1818).

This pivotal moment in Mary Shelley's story occurs when Victor Frankenstein, choosing to cross over the boundary between life and death, says he will "pour a torrent of light into our dark world" (Shelley, 1818). In this moment, he not only anoints himself as a new creator god, he also changes the parameters between life and death in a fundamental way, which has had prophetic implications that linger with us today. Death is a matter of fact, and as such the value of life is changed.

Death as a measure of life

Regarded as a matter of fact, death is the event that takes the measure of life, and as such life itself can be translated into an event. As events, death and life can be regarded as only biological processes and both of these moments lose their meanings as human experiences.[2] Thus, when Victor Frankenstein commits himself to overcoming death as an inevitable human fate, he begins with observing the steps through which the body decays. In this part of Mary Shelley's story, we begin to see Victor Frankenstein as a man whose cold logic has distanced him from the human experience of death. In his wish to defeat the "Great Spoiler" Victor Frankenstein is becoming a spectator mind, whose origins, which I have described elsewhere, are rooted in the fifteenth century creation of the scientific method.[3]

From this distance, *no one* dies. In this regard, Victor does not so much triumph over death; he does not defeat the Great Spoiler. Rather, he changes the terms of his question by shifting his attitude toward death.

But what might Victor have discovered if he began his work by recognizing that the dualism of death and life ignores life as the pivot between birth and death. As a pivot, life is not measured by death. Death is not just a biological event, something that just happens to no one in particular. As a pivot, life turns round the moments of birth and death, and, in these turnings, life as it is being lived takes up each of them, endowing each with a human significance. For example, birth is remembered by celebrations of one's birthday and death by rituals of mourning. In addition, on gravestones the passage of someone's life is marked between the dates of his or her birth and death.

Living life between birth and death no longer necessarily places death at the end of the line. However, when and if one regards death as the period at the end of the life sentences that weave the stories of a life, then death is the end of the line. In this context, who would not applaud the noble attempt of Victor Frankenstein to defeat death? But, then, does not life itself become a flight from death filled with worry of its anticipation warded off by frantic efforts to delay the end as long as possible?

This is Victor's view and it does shape his own obsessive and, as he himself describes, at times frantic behavior. It is, in fact, a view at the very start of his work, present in the charnel houses where death as a biological event has already been stripped of its human meanings. Victor enters such houses of decay and death where those who are dead are in his eyes "no one."

But what if a person is able to regard death as the last word in the narrative of his or her life? Then does death as the measure of life step back a bit to become the word that gives one's life its meaning? This shift does not cancel out the sorrow of dying, but it does offer another view. As a measure of life, as the period at the end of the sentence, as a biological event death is *what* happens. As an experience that shapes the course of a person's life lived between birth and death, as the last word in the story of someone's life, *how* someone lives into his or her dying matters.

Living life between birth and death changes our relation to time. Time becomes not just a line of progress or decay. Living life between birth and death, one lives within the spiral of time in which every present moment offers the possibility of remembering what has been in light of what might be and vice versa: To remember the past is to re-member it in light of a future that is imagined; to imagine a future in light of a past that is re-membered is for oneself to be re-membered. Each present moment, then, is a way of creating one's life, of re-creating it. Each present moment in the spiral of time as we live it is the possibility of a symbolic resurrection.[4]

But this is not the resurrection that Victor Frankenstein desires. It is not the desire at the core of his dream because it cannot be. He does not live in a world where time spirals between birth and death. He lives in a world where time leads only to death, where death at the end of the line is a biological termination, where, as the Great Spoiler, Death destroys life. Within this context, Victor's dream of resurrection is one engineered by man, a resurrection of the dead into the paradise of scientific and technological powers and wonders. In this context, resurrection as a renewal of life becomes the literal re-animation of dead flesh.

Because Victor Frankenstein takes the measure of life from the side of death, because he understands death as just a material event, there is no place for birth in his project. If he creates a way in which no one has to die, he also creates a way in which no one is born. As a new creator god, Victor Frankenstein is a version of the patriarchal Christian creator god, who creates life apart from the feminine. Conceiving his creature in the convoluted caverns of his own mind, and gestating it for two years, his work exemplifies and anticipates that type of spectator mind split off from the feminine. But is it correct to say that no one is born of this unnatural act?[5]

Mary Shelley's story is a cautionary tale and in fact something is born of Victor Frankenstein's work. But what is born of his work apart from the feminine is monstrous, which adds to the caution a prophetic dimension. To understand those prophetic amplifications, we need first to dig a bit more deeply into the grounds of Victor's work.

The charnel house

A charnel house is a house of death and it is to such a place that Victor repeatedly goes to observe the forces of decay, to chart the steps through which flesh rots and falls away. It is also the place where he begins to collect some of the materials for his studies, the bones and muscles, eyes and organs that comprise the fabric of the anatomical body. In this regard, Victor is at work in that place already made possible by the anatomical gaze that began in the sixteenth century with Andreas Vesalius who dissected his way into the body and then drew from within its cavernous openings the first textbook in modern anatomy.[6]

Victor is drawn to this place of corruption and decay, and it is ironic that he tells this part of his tale to Captain Robert Walton. In Mary Shelley's story, Walton is the one who, after rescuing Frankenstein from the icy Arctic waters as he is pursuing his monster in order to kill him, tells Victor's story in a series of letters to his sister. These encounters between Walton and Frankenstein have an ironic edge because as he is telling Walton about his dream and his work to banish death from life, Frankenstein himself is dying. Given his belief that death is merely a biological event, is he indifferent to his own death in these final moments of his life? Or, is there a dim glimmer of recognition of the difference between his own death and his ideas about death as a biological event?

A clue to an answer to these questions can be found in his description of his work to Captain Walton:

> Who shall conceive the horrors of my secret toil, as I dabbled among the unhallowed damps of the grave, or tortured the living animal to animate the lifeless clay? I collected bones from charnel houses; and disturbed with profane fingers, the tremendous secrets of the human frame. In a solitary chamber, or rather cell, at the top of the house, and separated from all the other apartments by a gallery and staircase, I kept my workshop of filthy creation. The dissecting room and the slaughter house furnished many of my materials.
>
> (Shelley, 1818)

Isolating himself in his cell, as he calls his work place, the tone of Victor's tale to Walton suggests that his dream of creating life where death has taken hold appears to have distanced him from the existential reality of his own death. Consumed by the possibility that he can succeed and driven forward by "a resistless, and almost frantic impulse," his work has become an obsession. He tells Walton he is forced to enter these houses of the dead, these vaults of decay and corruption. In his obsession, even while his own human nature did often fill him with loathing for the work he was doing, he did not allow such natural feelings to stand in his way.

But if we allow ourselves to enter through his words into these places of decaying and rotting flesh with all their noxious odors, we might begin to understand what Victor's dream has done to him. We might realize that Victor Frankenstein has become the very thing he is studying. There in the charnel houses and digging with his fingers into the rotting flesh of the a body he is already dead. He has, as he says, "lost all soul and sensation but for this one pursuit" (Shelley, 1818). He confesses that all the aesthetic charms and appeals of the natural world have become so distant to him that they no longer distract him from his focused vision. He has already become monstrous in a way, someone who no longer recognizes that the body that observes the body as a thing, as a specimen, is not identical with the body being observed. Possessed by the dreams of his Prometheus Project as it might be called, enthralled by the leaps of his daring work, Victor Frankenstein no longer sees the differences between the eye that sees the eye as a material object and the eye as seen in that way.[7]

What will emerge from the darkness of these charnel houses where death has taken life's measure?

To reply to that question requires a slight detour to the moon and its dark, soft light. From charnel houses to churchyard cemeteries moonlight guides the way. Moreover, as we shall see, the moon's dark light plays an important role in Mary Shelley's story. Not only does moonlight awaken Victor, at least for a moment, to the monstrous side of his dream of becoming a new creator god, it is in moonlight that we catch a glimpse of the beauty of the Monster.

Moon dust—1969

At a NASA press conference on the eve of the first moon landing in 1969, a reporter asked what could be heard as a frivolous question. He asked if NASA was concerned about the ability of the moon surface to support the weight of the lunar lander. Would the lander sink under its own weight?

From a scientific and technical point of view, of course, it was not at all a frivolous concern. It was also not a reasonable worry because geological evidence indicated that the moon surface would support the lander.

But that question was and is remarkable because what bubbles up from its surface is a fundamental human experience. Rising up from below, the question reminds us that our Promethean leap into space has changed something we naturally assume and take for granted: the ground on which we stand and have always stood, the ground of Earth where we bury the dead. The dead under-stand us; they stand under us; we stand upon and count on the dead for their support. No humans had died on the moon and no humans were buried there.

In preparation for the first moon landing, does the question about the moon's ground bring to the surface of the collective imagination how Earth as our ground has changed?

Does that question awaken a doubt about how we are continuing Victor Frankenstein's Prometheus Project?

Is his Prometheus Project without a stable human ground?

Is death as the measure of life shaky ground for the spectator mind's dream of becoming a new creator god?

Churchyard cemeteries

From observation to experimentation, Victor moves stealthily and in moonlight from the charnel houses of death to churchyard cemeteries where the dead supposedly rest. But his vision of this place has already been radically altered.

The churchyard cemetery, the ground of Victor's work, is not for him sacred ground, the ground where the rituals of burial and the rites of mourning are enacted. This ground where he digs up the material for his work is unhallowed ground. This ground, which has become for him merely a receptacle for bodies that have been deprived of life, is no longer a tomb for the dead. It is a container for material that has no life. In this ground where death has become the measure of life, the dead have become a resource.

Remembering the dead

More than two decades ago I had a powerful experience of the persistence of memory and its relation to the dead. It took place in a cemetery on a hill overlooking a small town to which I was drawn as I was making my way to the airport of a major city in the southwest United States. I was going to be late and I was in a hurry, but something made me detour along a side road toward the cemetery.

Even now in this unplanned detour away from the narrative of this book, I still hear the keening sounds of the rusted iron gates as they move in the strong wind. Today I can still see the tumbleweeds that drift amidst the un-flowered graves. A sad loneliness hovers again in the air where the names and dates of those who lie here are becoming illegible.

As I did then I know now that no one is ever really dead until one's name has been forgotten. No one is ever really dead until there is no one left to remember that person.

Memory is born at the site of the grave where we come together to bury a dead person, someone with a name and a history. We do not come together to bury a corpse. We gather together to mourn someone who has died. We do not come together to mourn no one or anyone. We inscribe headstones with the names of those who have died. We do not inscribe headstones with the names of no one or anyone. At the site of the grave we bear witness to the belief that the dead go on in some way. Collectively we perform the time honored rites and rituals that are symbolic modes of resurrection.

Victor Frankenstein's work belongs to an age that believes science and technology are ushering in an age of progress. That belief goes hand in hand with Frankenstein's view of those churchyard cemeteries as receptacles for bodies that have been deprived of life. For him *no one* is buried there.

If memory is born at the site of the grave, do we in the age of progress even have time to mourn someone who has died?

In an age of progress where what lies ahead is approaching us at ever increasing speed, can we even take time to remember?

Do Victor Frankenstein's dream and his work sever the bonds between memory and the dead?

What happens to the dead if they no longer live in our memories?

And what happens to us if we no longer stand upon their ground?

Galileo in church

Haunting churchyard cemeteries, Victor Frankenstein is treading new ground that was already being prepared in the late sixteenth century when Galileo works out the laws of pendulum motion while attending Mass in church. Counting the pulse beats of his heart, which is a vision of the heart as a pump that Vesalius had described a century earlier, Galileo times the arc of the lighted lamp that marks the presence of Christ in the tabernacle. Crossing the threshold between the secular world of everyday life and the world of the sacred, Galileo also crosses the boundary between the human world and the world of the gods. He makes his own Promethean leap in the experiment he performs. He is no longer a member of the worshiping community. He is the spectator mind for whom the human body has become a material object in service to his experiment and for whom the sacred lamp is being made into a scientific instrument. The lamp is no longer part of a ritual space. It is a spectacle whose motions are to be observed and measured.

Victor Frankenstein is a new creator god who uses the powers of the new science of electricity to engineer a non-symbolic kind of resurrection of the dead. Displacing death from its sacred ground to the new ground of the laboratory, a new paradise where the ancient dream of immortality is promised, he cuts the bond between death and the sacred.

What happens to us if we make ourselves the measure of life?

What happens to us when the sacred is no longer a measure that sets the boundary of human life?

Who are we when the bonds that have tied us to the dead and the bonds that have obligated us to the gods have been broken?[8]

When Victor Frankenstein conceives his dream, these questions are not yet asked. When he makes death the measure of life, they hover in the background of his work. When he walks from the holy ground of the churchyard cemetery to his filthy cell of creation as he calls it, the questions are drawing closer to him. And when he digs up one of those anonymous corpses from that unholy ground, takes it to his laboratory, sparks life into it and sees a pale yellow eye of his creature staring at him, the questions take on a face and a form. Victor Frankenstein and the Monster, the thing he has made and will then abandon, a being who is never named and who has never had the proper rituals of burial and mourning, are doomed to haunt the living with these questions.

Frankenstein as Prophecy

Haunted by death

Victor Frankenstein's wish to erase Death as the Spoiler of life is a project born in Mary Shelley's dream. But the death that would be exiled from life lives on in his work, and Death the Spoiler haunts his life.

On a dreary November night, having worked for nearly two years to the detriment of his own health, Victor looks upon his creation. The lifeless thing lies at his feet. A dismal rain slaps at his window. As he looks down on the creature, he sees in the flickering light of his nearly extinguished candle the dull pale yellow eyes open. Recoiling at the sight, horrified by what he sees, he rushes from the laboratory and flees to his bedroom. Agitated and exhausted, he finally succumbs to sleep. But his sleep is disturbed by a dream:

> I thought I saw Elizabeth, in the bloom of health, walking in the streets of Ingolstadt. Delighted and surprised I embraced her; but as I imprinted the first kiss on her lips, they became livid with the hue of death; her features appeared to change, and I thought I held the corpse of my dead mother in my arms; a shroud enveloped her form, and I saw the grave worms crawling in the folds of the flannel.
>
> *(Shelley, 1818)*[9]

The very first fruits of Victor's Prometheus Project that would be the death of death are spoiled. They burst forth in a nightmare suffused with decay and corruption. Death, the Spoiler, already claims Elizabeth Lavenza, Victor's childhood friend and his wife to be. The kiss of life and love has already become the kiss of death. This nightmarish dream image is the first monstrous face of Victor Frankenstein's Prometheus Project.

The first victim of the hubris of Victor's dream to become a god capable of creating life is his young brother William, who is accidently murdered when he encounters the Monster while walking in the woods near his home. When Victor hears the news of William's death, he knows in his heart that his Monster has done it, but he denies it to himself, trying to convince himself that it is not possible. He also keeps silent when Justine Moritz is accused of the murder. A faithful servant of the Frankenstein household and even regarded as part of the Frankenstein family she is condemned by Victor's silence and denial and is hanged. Later, after Victor has destroyed the mate he was creating for his Monster, whose loneliness touched for a brief moment Victor's heart, the Monster murders Victor's lifelong friend and companion Henry Clerval and vows to be with Victor on his own wedding night. Enmeshed in the narcissism of his own Promethean hubris, Victor is unable to understand that the threat is not aimed at him but at his intended bride, Elizabeth. And indeed, it is she who falls victim to the death that would be denied. His nightmare has happened. Victor's father, consumed by the grief of all these deaths, also dies of a broken heart.

Recounting these events to Captain Walton as he himself is dying, Victor seems to realize the insane folly of his work. Responding to Walton's interest and curiosity, he shouts, "Are you mad, my friend?" His question reveals what he has already come to know. With all the deaths that have followed in the wake of his dream to remove the stain of death from life, "The cup of life was poisoned forever" (Shelley, 1818).

Death the Spoiler has become the spoiler of life!

But whose life is spoiled?

Victor's life?

Only his life?

A hundred years after Frankenstein's nightmare, the battle of the Somme begins on July 1, 1916. By the time it is over on November 18 over one million soldiers have died. It is the most destructive battle ever fought in all human history.

The cup of life spoiled by Death the Spoiler has expanded in scope and ferocity. The Promethean Mind that would be the death of death has become its agent:

Six million Jews among countless others exterminated in the Holocaust!

A hundred thousand killed instantly by one bomb on August 6, 1945 in Hiroshima, not to mention all those others who would suffer the lethal effects of radiation poisoning, and those killed three days later in Nagasaki in the second display of the Promethean power that stole the fires of the sun to unleash on Earth.

The numbers stagger the imagination to such a depth that a new word had to be created to describe these horrors: Genocide. The term coined by Raphael Lemkin in 1944 was adopted in 1948 by the newly formed United Nations in the Convention on the Prevention and Punishment of the Crime of Genocide.

Whose life has been poisoned?

Do we avoid drinking from that cup when we imagine that the very same Prometheus Project that has poisoned life will find the antidote?

Do we believe that the cup that has been poisoned has been drained by these events that happened before, taking refuge in the fantasy that time is a line, that what is past is past and best forgotten, that we have progressed beyond these horrors?

But the events seem not to end. They seem to go on, even as valiant attempts are made not to forget or deny their occurrence. The poison has become stronger and the Promethean Mind a more efficient agent in service to the Great Spoiler Death that Victor Frankenstein dreamed of vanquishing:

Cambodia, 1975–1979: approximately 3,000,000 Cambodians, between 21% and 33% of the population, exterminated!

Rwanda, 1994: between 500,000 and 1,000,000 Tutsis, approximately 70% of them, exterminated!

Darfur, 2003: 300,000 Darfuri civilians exterminated!

Have we all become madmen?

The Monster and the madman

In 1882 Friedrich Nietzsche proclaims the death of God in *The Gay Science*. The decree is however more famously associated with the character of the "Madman" in *Thus Spoke Zarathustra* published in 1883.

> God is dead. God remains dead. And we have killed him. How shall we comfort ourselves, the murderers of all murderers? What was holiest and mightiest of all that the world has yet owned has bled to death under our knives: who will wipe this blood off us? What water is there for us to clean ourselves? What festivals of atonement, what sacred games shall we have to invent? Is not the greatness of this deed too great for us? Must we ourselves now become gods simply to appear worthy of it?
>
> *(Kaufmann, 1959, pp. 93–94)*

Could not Victor Frankenstein have also proclaimed God is dead?

Are not those words the heart of Victor's Prometheus Project to become a new god?

Does Victor know that he has killed God?

As he goes about his Promethean task nothing in his work suggests that the death of God is his intention. It is the death of death that he seeks and yet with the surgical knives he uses to create the body of his Monster, the Christian God does bleed to death.

Nietzsche's "Madman" worries about our blood soaked hands and wonders if any rituals of atonement are possible. He even wonders if the death of God is too far beyond us, if it has exceeded all human boundaries.

Only once does Victor pause, and then very briefly, to consider if he should take on the work of creating life, which for countless ages has been the work of the gods. And when he crosses that boundary between humanity and the gods and takes on the mantle of becoming a god, he believes his intentions would be an achievement for which all humankind will praise him. The death of death is an unalloyed good. The death of God is the price to be paid for the death of death.

To be worthy of the death of God, Victor Frankenstein has to become a god himself.

Is the violent terrorism of our god wars a price we are paying today for acting as if we are gods?

The twin towers, Al Qaeda, Isis, as well as the ongoing struggle between Palestinians and Jews are political and economic battles which have their tap roots in religious ideology. These god wars are a prophetic expression of the Promethean

Mind's erasure of the boundary between humanity and the gods. They are the disguised forms of the monsters made on the margins of the Promethean Mind, a global expression of madness sourced in part as a reaction to the secularization of a technological world that can seem inhuman in its scale, an un-world, whose globalization is often economically and ecologically destructive and whose bottom line corporate policies and bureaucratic indifference trump local concerns and ecological boundaries.

The Prometheus Project is the myth of our age and its monstrous faces are beginning to show on the margins. AIDS, SARS and the Zika virus, for example, which were previously contained within their ecological boundaries, are the ways in which Frankenstein's abandoned Monster haunts us as prophecy. They now crisscross the world bringing disease and death to ever larger numbers. Prometheus today not only crosses boundaries, he rides above them.

As the myth of our age, the Promethean Project is spawning fear and regressive returns to political, economic, social and especially religious forms of fundamentalism. As the rate and scope of change in technology increasingly outpace our social, economic and political institutions, the intolerance at the core of all forms of fundamentalism show the destructive consequences of our unchecked use of our god like powers.

The god of matter

When humanity takes on the role of being god, the Promethean Mind without any boundaries knows no bounds. But our flesh mocks that Promethean Mind. We eat and at times we ache. We grow weary and need to rest. We age and we die. The human body is a humiliation to the wish to be a god. Victor's Monster in his disfigured form is the emblem of that humiliation.

For Victor Frankenstein the human body is the primary impediment to his dream to raise the dead. To overcome that obstacle, Frankenstein transforms living flesh into raw material. A man of his time well suited to the exciting developments of the industrial revolution, Victor Frankenstein is a materialist who worships at the altar of matter.

These rituals of worship are at the heart of the new science described in the sixteenth century by Francis Bacon. Nature, he is reported to have said, is to be put upon the rack so that her secrets can be tortured from her. For the Promethean Mind worshiping at the altar of matter, the spirit of nature tortured on the rack is identified with the feminine. The living Spirit of Nature is made into a servant to satisfy the needs of human kind. The body of Mother Nature is to be ravished as resources for our use and abuse. The death that would be tamed casts its shadows over the world of nature.

But the shadows cast over the world of nature as well as the shadow forms of the human body as a material object now made ready for multiple transformation from Monster to Cyborg and beyond are themes for subsequent questions.

So we take leave of Victor Frankenstein in the churchyard cemeteries and charnel houses with a sense of something vital to a full human life, which, although buried and forgotten, lingers on the margins of the spectator mind. Although the intimacy of embodiment and our ties to nature are becoming more and more strange to us, although we are becoming aliens, as it were, in this new paradise of material progress, although there are increasing moments when we might glimpse in the faces of the escalating number of refugees our own sense of homelessness, these prophecies are not yet our fate. As long as the capacity to question remains, the possibility of change remains.[10]

Notes

1 Where it is suitable I use the present tense when speaking of historical events and fictional characters in order to underscore that Mary Shelley's story as well as the characters of Victor Frankenstein and the Monster have not only endured but also are psychologically alive in the collective cultural imagination. While Mary Shelley's story was finished in 1818, it was not done. It continues to be written. *The Frankenstein Prophecies* is part of this process.

  In this context, while my approach in *The Frankenstein Prophecies* follows the argument I made about psychological writing in *The Wounded Researcher* (2007), it was Susan Rowland, the Jung scholar and writer, who deepened that argument by drawing my attention to Carl Jung's discussion of visionary creativity. I am indebted to her for helping me see not only that Mary Shelley's story is an excellent illustration of a visionary work of art, but also how the style of *The Frankenstein Prophecies* has implicitly drawn on Jung's idea.

  In her remarkable book *Jung as a Writer* (2005), Rowland not only unfolds the radical contributions for literary studies of Jung's style as a writer, she also shows how his idea of visionary creativity can address contemporary crises. "A visionary work," she says, "may detect the obscure traces of what is yet to come" (p. 196). It also plays a "compensatory role to the historical conditions of its time ... and represents a teleological movement towards future social processes" (p. 210).

  Reading Mary Shelley's story as prophecy detects what is yet on the way. *The Frankenstein Prophecies* also shows how the prophetic character of her story compensates the cultural and historical contexts of Victor Frankenstein's work and how it foreshadows contemporary technological, political and social crises. In addition, Rowland describes how Jung's reading of James Joyce's *Ulysses* was a traumatic event, and in this context my own multiple readings of Mary Shelley's story was a traumatic encounter with the Monster and his tale. Faced with the Monster, the format of questions was a way in which I could let myself be addressed by the Monster on the margins without being overwhelmed by his descendants lingering in the shadows of our collective psyche in the guise of symptoms, haunting the margins of the collective mind in various monstrous forms. Indeed, this format gave me some room to see seeds of hope in Mary Shelley's story, to be present to the Monster and his tale, to see through the horror of the story its redemptive possibilities. In this regard, reading Mary Shelley's story as a visionary work of art can have therapeutic value. As such, it underscores the contributions of and the vital necessity for visionary works of art to communal life in times of political, economic and psychological upheavals.

2 For an excellent example of the difference between life as a biological event and as a human experience with its varied meanings see J. H. van den Berg *The Psychology of the Sickbed* (1966).

3 I describe the spectator mind in my book, *Technology as Symptom and Dream* (1989/ 2006). In it I showed how the fifteenth century development of linear perspective vision was an artistic invention to reproduce on the flat surface of a canvas the illusion of depth. Essential to that technique, the onlooker had to be imagined as if he were behind

a window, which eventually was transformed into a gridded screen. That artistic invention became over time a cultural convention, a habit of mind according to which the human subject could best know the world by distancing himself or herself from it. It was a new way of knowing and being in the world that laid the foundations for the modern scientific and technological world-view, and which eventually eclipsed the medieval world-view. In radical and fundamental ways, that artistic invention transformed our sense of nature, our relation to the body and the world, and was the beginning of the eclipse of the sacred and the death of God.

As the onlooker behind the window slowly became a disembodied spectator mind, the human body a specimen probed and dissected in the new science of anatomy pioneered by Andreas Vesalius, and the world a spectacle, an inanimate object for our use and abuse, the historical seeds of Victor Frankenstein's work were planted. Indeed, these events made Mary Shelley's story not only possible, but perhaps also necessary. It is as if those events came to life in her story and now live on in the collective, cultural imagination.

4 I am not speaking here of the Christian sense of resurrection. Rather I am speaking of it as a psychological belief in the possibility of renewal, which is at the core of those moments when, for example, one feels a sense of hope about starting over again. In like manner I am not speaking about religion when I use the term God. Rather I am speaking psychologically about God as a *limit* that frames the human condition. For a good example of this difference between a religious and a psychological perspective regarding god see Carl Jung, *Answer to Job* (1958/1973).

5 The term spectator mind, as well as its counterparts specimen body and spectacle world are codes whose origins are tied to the invention of linear perspective ways of knowing and being in the world. Their meanings have so deeply penetrated the cultural imagination that they have become archetypal motifs. Initially, I used capital letters for each of them to call our attention to how, in becoming archetypal motifs in the collective imagination, they have moved beyond the cultural and historical moments of their origins. But some early readers of my manuscript suggested it interrupted the narrative flow of the book. For details about the three terms see note three above.

6 For Vesalius see note three above.

7 This power of the human body to take up its biological conditions and transform them into intentional acts of meaning is the core of Maurice Merleau-Ponty's philosophy. For a detailed description of his work see *The Structure of Behavior* (1942/1963), *Phenomenology of Perception* (1945/1962) and *The Visible and the Invisible* (1968). See also my essays, "The Body in Psychotherapy: Contributions of Merleau-Ponty" (2011) and "The Body as Historical Matter and Cultural Symptom" (1992).

8 Victor Frankenstein is truly a modern Prometheus. Like his mythological forebear his work is done in service to humankind. There are, however, two significant differences between the mythic figure of Prometheus and the fictional character of Victor Frankenstein: First, Prometheus's story takes place within a sacred cosmos where the gods are real presences. In his service to humankind he therefore goes against the gods. Victor Frankenstein's story unfolds within a secular world in which he is a new god; Second, it is Prometheus who suffers for transgressing the boundaries between the gods and humankind. While Victor Frankenstein suffers for his hubris, his work also brings on suffering for many others. The cup of life, as he says, is spoiled but it is spoiled not only for him, but also for us who are living within his secular version of the Promethean story.

9 Fifty years before the birth of Freud in 1856 Mary Shelley already anticipates some major themes in psychoanalysis. In this dream she already suggests what Freud will later call the Oedipus complex. But I would not wish to reduce her vision to an interpretation. Rather I am suggesting only that she is part of that Romantic tradition of Freud's work, which values dream, night, the animated spirit of nature and the imagination. In addition, since much of *The Frankenstein Prophecies* adopts the archetypal perspective of Jungian psychology, this dream suggests that she intuited how Victor Frankenstein as a patriarchal expression of the Solar Mind is dominated by the absence of the mother, or one might even say the dead mother. Consider that Victor's work begins with his refusal

or inability to grieve the death of his mother, and, as if in reaction to that trauma, he creates life without any participation of the feminine. In addition, two key feminine figures in the novel—Elizabeth Lavenza and Justine Moritz—are sacrificed to his work. Moreover, when he realizes in horror through the light of the moon what he has done and is doing again as he is making a mate for the Monster he tears her to pieces. Indeed, this archetypal theme of the masculine solar mind split off from the feminine lunar light is threaded through Mary Shelley's story and finds a key place in *The Frankenstein Prophecies*.

10 It is an established fact of depth psychology that the monsters we create through our denial of responsibilities for our actions do live on in our dreams, fantasies and symptoms, as well as in the projections of them onto others in order to trump them. The monsters we make live on as emblems of humiliation. As such, they humble us if and when we can face them. Indeed, this is the key theme of this book, and, as I have been writing it, I am reminded daily of the fact that while this lesson in humiliation is so difficult for each of us individually, it seems almost impossible for us collectively. And yet despite the difficulty, given our technological capacities for destruction, it is now necessary to take up this challenge if we are to survive.

Question Two

THE MELTING POLAR ICE

Is Mary Shelley's story a prophecy of the dying of nature? [1]

He works continuously, feverishly, often without sleep for long periods of time, consumed as he is with his project to create life. For two years he shuts himself off from family and friends and most of all from Elizabeth Lavenza, his wife to be. Now almost in despair he feels he has failed, for the thing that he has worked so laboriously to infuse with the spark of life lies lifeless on the laboratory table.

Exhausted, he falls into sleep. But soon Victor Frankenstein is disturbed and awakened by the thing he has made. His dream has been realized.

In the fragile, wispy fabric of the dream, this moment weaves us among Mary Shelley, Victor Frankenstein and the Monster. Just as Victor Frankenstein was born from Mary Shelley's waking dream, the Monster has been born from his maker's dream to create life, which we are still dreaming.

Has the thing itself been dreaming as he stirred into life, dreaming on the edge of that previously impassable boundary between death and life?

Might it have been as much his dream as it was the spark of electricity that awakened him into life?

What dream might the Monster have been dreaming?

Have we come to know his dream as our nightmare?

Conceived by man, not born of woman

This thing with no name, this thing that will never be named by his creator but only labeled as monster, devil and demon, is an abomination of nature. No womb has housed and protected his fragile being. He will not suckle at a mother's breast nor ever be nourished by a mother's milk. A mother's arms will never cradle him in his sorrows, nor will a mother's eyes ever grace him with a loving regard. Never will he hear a mother's voice whisper words of comfort. Never will he hear a mother's song to soothe his troubled heart.

Perhaps this motherless thing called monster by his creator and abandoned by him foresees in his dream that he is to be also without a mate.

Perhaps he fears a life of utter loneliness.

Is that the destiny for him of his unnatural birth, a thing born of his creator's Promethean Mind, whose very being is so out of touch with the natural order of things that he is condemned to wander forever alone and in exile, an outcast from the human community?

Is the nightmarish quality of such an existence what shocks him into life?

It is unbearable and now on the day of his birth does he already conceive his plan to appeal to his creator to make him a mate to assuage his loneliness?

Death in moonlight[2]

Even the first Adam had his Eve to assuage his loneliness, but the Monster has no feminine companion. In his loneliness he appeals several times to his maker to create a mate for him but Victor continuously refuses, horrified at the possibility of creating another monstrous thing. In time however, even Victor, who has been deaf all along to any of the Monster's appeals, is moved by the sorrow of the Monster. Acknowledging, at least for a moment, that he does have obligations to the thing he has made, Victor assents to his request. But Victor sets one condition and exacts from the Monster a binding promise:

> I consent to your demand, on your solemn oath to quit Europe forever, and every other place in the neighbourhood of man, as soon as I shall deliver into your hands a female who will accompany you in your exile.
>
> *(Shelley, 1818)*

Already alone and in exile, the Monster readily agrees to Victor's demand. In his brief and miserable existence is this the first time the Monster knows the human experience of hope? Perhaps there will be an Eve for him as there was for the first Adam.

His hope, however, is not to be fulfilled.

Sometime later Victor begins his journey to the wild highlands of northern Scotland where he intends to begin the work of making a mate for the Monster. And yet even as he travels toward the place where he will fulfill his promise, his soul is being gnawed by a sense of his own despair. Describing this moment in his story to Captain Walton, the image of the blasted tree trunk comes to mind. That event, which figured so prominently in his youthful imagination about one day harnessing the destructive powers of nature to create life, now becomes an emblem of his misery:

> But I am a blasted tree; the bolt has entered my soul; and I felt then that I should survive to exhibit, what I shall soon cease to be—a miserable spectacle of wrecked humanity, pitiable to others, and abhorrent to myself.
>
> *(Shelley, 1818)*

In this reflection is he describing only himself, or is he also describing the Monster he has created and abandoned?

In this brief moment do we catch a glimpse of the kinship between Victor Frankenstein and the Monster he made, the doubling between the creator god and his abandoned creation, each pitiable to others, and abhorrent to themselves?

In this momentary pause along his journey is there for Victor Frankenstein some dim recognition that the Monster is not other to himself, some dawning but intolerable awareness that he has become the very thing he has made?

Perhaps, in this brief descent into his misery Victor Frankenstein is confronted for the first time with the question, "Who is the Monster?"

As if pulled by unseen forces, Victor Frankenstein finally arrives at the place where he will begin his second act of creation. But he is slow to begin his work. The manic fury that drove the first act of creation is absent, and for days at a time he abandons his laboratory and wanders the wild and windy hills of the Scottish landscape, as if trying to escape his troublesome task. Doubt is increasingly worming its way into his Promethean Mind, eroding the dream he once had of becoming a new kind of god who would free life from the Spoiler, Death.

Here in his own words spoken to Walton is a description of his state of mind:

> as I proceeded in my labour, it became every day more horrible and irksome to me. Sometimes I could not prevail on myself to enter my laboratory for several days; and at other times I toiled day and night to complete my work. It was indeed a filthy process in which I was engaged. During my first experiment, a kind of enthusiastic frenzy had blinded me to the horror of my employment … . But now I went to it in cold blood, and my heart often sickened at the work of my hands.
>
> *(Shelley, 1818)*

Eventually as the work is near completion he is overwhelmed again with the horror of what he has done and is now about to do to fulfill his promise to the Monster. As the moon is rising he catches sight of the Monster bathed in moonlight standing outside the window. In moonlight the promised mate, Victor and the Monster are drawn together.

She lies on the table, a feminine counterpart to the Monster Victor had made.

But what do Victor and the Monster see in moonlight?

For the Monster her disfigured form so like his own is no obstacle to his quickening hope and perhaps even joy. But for Victor there is no joy, there is only despair. In the full light of the moon his dream becomes a nightmare. The feminine mate he would make for his Monster awakens Victor to the monstrous shadows of his own mind. Until this moment those monstrous images were placed on his Monster, carved into his disfigured flesh. But now in moonlight, She mirrors Victor's own tortured and corrupted heart.[3] In moonlight She is a reminder of the perverse act he has committed against nature in conceiving life apart from woman. Life and death as only an ideal boundary that he could and would abolish by pouring a torrent of light onto the dark world of death is now mocked by her still and lifeless form.

But moonlight, so different than the solar light of Victor's Promethean Mind, which had excluded woman from the generative act of procreation, and which has guided his work, is too much for him to bear. This softer, darker light of the moon, which in so many of our myths and stories is linked to the feminine qualities of mind, is the shadow of the light of Victor's Promethean Mind. She is the nightmarish countenance of his wildly speculative dreams.

In his terror Victor wonders what might happen if She were now to draw her first breath. If She were to come to life would the Monster keep his promise to quit the neighborhoods of mankind forever? Or, would they propagate and in producing offspring fill the world with a race of devils that would terrorize the heart of humanity and even imperil its existence?

Moonlight, lunar light, lunacy now bewitches Victor. The dead woman in moonlight drives him mad. As his Monster watches in horror and disbelief, Victor aborts her creation. Descending into a fury of malicious destruction, he rips her form to pieces to be thrown later into a deep, cold Scottish lake where She will sink into oblivion, into an unmarked grave where no rituals of mourning will ever be performed.

The Monster now knows that unlike any creature that has a mate, he forevermore will be alone. His wretched isolation is now complete and only one act remains for him when his one hope has been destroyed. As rage replaces his sorrow he vows that Victor will, like himself, never know happiness or peace. The torrent of light that Victor had dreamed of pouring into the dark corners of death will now with every morning sunrise shed light only on his maker's misery. Facing his creator, the Monster addresses him generically, as if it is not only the person of Victor who will pay for his crime, but all of humanity, who share the hubris of the Promethean Mind that would play at being a god who would erase death from life:

Man, you shall repent of the injuries you inflict.

(Shelley, 1818)

Pausing for only a breath, he promises that he will be with Victor on his wedding night.

The wedding night

He will be with his maker on his wedding night. This threat by the Monster to visit vengeance on his creator is a pivot where the tale of Victor and his Monster turns back upon itself. Now the Monster who was born of man and man alone becomes the agent of destruction. A blind and ruthless force of nature as it were, the Monster murders Elizabeth Lavenza, his maker's mate to be, on their wedding night. It is an action that mirrors Victor's crime against nature, when he dreamed of being a god who would exclude woman from the creative act of procreation. It is an act that reveals the price to be paid for Victor's hubris. Elizabeth Lavenza, lying dead on her wedding bed, is the double of the Monster's mate torn to pieces on Victor's laboratory table. Elizabeth Lavenza is the shadow of the Monster's aborted mate and together they display the discarded, excluded, exiled feminine as dead.

Is the dead woman the price exacted by the god like hubris of the Promethean Mind?[4]

Who lies in that watery grave where Frankenstein rid himself of the Monster's mate that he destroyed?

As her shadow image might Elizabeth Lavenza reflect something of her? If she does, then we can imagine that She who lies in that unmarked grave would be like Elizabeth.

But who is Elizabeth Lavenza?

We know her only through Victor's eyes and perhaps the most specific sense we get of her is when Victor speaks of their youth to Captain Walton and draws this comparison:

> I delighted in investigating the facts of the actual world; she busied herself in following the aerial creations of the poets. The world was to me a secret, which I desired to discover; to her it was a vacancy, which she sought to people with imaginations of her own.
>
> *(Shelley, 1818)*

It seems a charming portrait, but it does depict her as naïve and even childlike, less a person in her own right and more a foil and even, as the wedding night shows, a sacrifice to Victor's life and work. So, Elizabeth never really lived just as the Monster's mate will never live. Both women are aborted, one quite physically and the other psychologically.

But, still, in the deep waters of her tomb does She have a name?

Victor's story is a re-telling of the Christian story of creation. He is a male creator god who engineers through the powers of science and technology a new resurrection. As such he not only repeats the exclusion of Woman from the act of creation, he repeats the Christian story within which Woman is the spoiler of creation. Just as Eve is at fault and is blamed for the fall from Paradise, the Monster's mate in moonlight spoils Victor's dream to be a new god. Death and Woman are identified in the spectator mind. Having omitted Woman in his first act of creation, Victor now destroys her presence in the second act.[5]

Perhaps, then, in the deep waters of her tomb the Monster's mate does have a name. Perhaps She is the new Eve, counterpart to the Monster as the new Adam.

Is that what Victor sees as he looks at her in moonlight?

In her disfigured form is She the image of the price to be paid for the dream of man and man alone to be the creator of life?

Abandoned and forgotten has She taken her story to the grave?

Neglected, does her story nevertheless go on, haunting us from those watery depths?

From her watery tomb is She the face and form of revenge of the murdered feminine?

Frankenstein as Prophecy

Nature on the rack

While it is questionable if Francis Bacon, sixteenth century visionary and prophet of the new sciences, actually said that the new sciences were to put nature on the rack to torture her secrets from her, the spirit of those words and that image have not been incompatible with the methods and development of science until more recent times.[6] The probing, questioning mode designed to force nature to answer the questions put to her has framed the dialogue for aspects of nature that could be measured. Power and domination over nature were at the heart of this method. Insofar as Bacon's alleged words identified nature with the feminine, this exercise of power and domination would apply to the feminine. They, like nature, were to speak only in reply to what was asked of them. Nature and the feminine lost their own autonomous voices.

Was the spirit of Bacon's words and their horrific image a condition that made Victor's dream possible?

Is Victor's laboratory table a form of that "rack"?

Have we become Nature's torturer?

Victor's dream begins in response to his mother's death. And his dream comes to its tragic ending with the murder of his beloved Elizabeth. But Death as the Spoiler he would banish from life returns. The new Eve, the aborted feminine, the dead woman in moonlight linger today in their prophetic presence as the dying of nature as we have come to know it.

Wild fires in California and other regions of the southwestern United States as well as in Australia and even in the Arctic Circle are becoming increasingly frequent and destructive!

The oceans of the world are becoming increasingly acidic and poisonous to many species of marine life, including the erosion of the Great Barrier Reef, the largest life form on Earth!

The rain forests of the Amazon, the lungs of the planet, are being sacrificed as resources for economic use and abuse!

Animal and plant species are disappearing in record numbers, as, for example, polar bears face an increasing loss of sea ice that is necessary for them to hunt for food!

The permafrost areas of the planet that are reservoirs of methane gas are melting at an alarming rate increasing global mean temperatures!

The facts are overwhelming and in their magnitude it often seems easier to turn away, to slip into some form of denial that would believe things cannot be that bad. But in 2017 the world witnessed catastrophic global weather events that were too shocking to ignore.

For example, Hurricane Harvey, which devastated Houston, Galveston, Corpus Christ and Port Arthur, Texas, was described as a storm that would happen maybe once every thousand years. But within days, Hurricane Irma, which followed Harvey, left Puerto Rico's infrastructure in near total ruin, and in that same week, storms left one-third of the nation of Bangledesh under water. A major factor in these storms is the increase in ocean temperature related to the atmospheric emissions released by fossil fuels.

Fossil fuels

The term fossil is part of the phrase fossil fuels that is so embedded in our global vocabulary that it rolls off the tongue without much thought. But as with all words there is or can be an image of its meaning, and in the context of Mary Shelley's story the image of a fossil plays a key role in Victor Frankenstein's dream.

A fossil is a piece of dead matter, the remains of decayed material of something that was once alive. It is a trace of an organism of some past geological age buried in nature. But whatever it is that is dead and buried, the word fossil refers specifically to what is to be or can be dug up. It is dead matter that is transformed into some use.

Its use is as fuel and in its many forms coal is the fossil that most fuels our energy economy. Our collective, global appetites for increasing amounts of energy are fueled by the dead. We dig deeply into nature to dig up the dead, decaying remains of what once was alive.

So does Victor Frankenstein! In churchyard cemeteries he digs up the dead remains of human beings to fuel his dream of creating life. The dead are of use to his work in transforming death into life.

Port Arthur, Texas

Port Arthur is the largest petro-chemical plant in the western hemisphere. It is a city whose refineries were created to change the fossil fuels ripped from the earth and the oceans into a saleable commodity. As such, it is a place where the climate crises of nature and our collective ravenous appetite for energy, coupled with the profit motive and greed of our capitalist, corporate culture, clash.[7]

Is Port Arthur, Texas, a place where Frankenstein's dream has become a fossil, where he and his work show themselves to be a way of life that is not only outdated, but also dangerous to nature and to us?

Are these monstrous storms the monster made by the hubris of the Promethean Mind playing god as it tortures nature's secrets from her?

Are these rains and flooding waters the Monster's mate rising up from her watery grave?

Are these storms the fury of the feminine that would no longer be silenced?

Is this the new normal that arises from nature on the rack, a new normal that is nerve racking?

When will it be enough for a sea change to happen, for another image other than the rack to rise up from the roiling waters?

Earthrise, 1968

On December 24, 1968 the Apollo 8 mission was in lunar orbit when astronaut Bill Anders took a photograph of Earth rising above the moon's surface into the black deep of space. It is an image that changed everything because for the first time in human history we were able to see the lonely beauty of our planet. From the distance of the moon the planet became an intimate home. Three years earlier the Russian cosmonaut, Alexei Leonov, who was the first human to walk in space, described the Earth as "Our home that must be defended like a holy relic" (quoted in Burnside, 2017, p. 55)

The irony of this image is that the technology that made it possible is also the technology that has racked nature. The crises of technology's Promethean dream are a danger and an opportunity. The opportunity of this image is that its frail beauty awakens a sense of the sacred, numinous dimension of nature so eclipsed in the materialism that has regarded nature as an inanimate resource for our use.

Such moments might seem like miracles, but they are open to each of us when and if we pause to be a witness to the extraordinary in the ordinary, the miracle in the mundane. Such moments are possible when and if we make a place for Elizabeth Lavenza, Victor's bride to be, whose imagination he only tolerated as a frivolous, feminine quality to fill the vacancy of nature.

An epiphany of wonder

Sitting in the garden of our house in Fanjeaux, a very small village in the Aude region of France, where I have come to write this book, I am thinking how this landscape and its light remind me of the paintings by the French Impressionists. Spellbound by the way in which nature displays itself in its stillness and quiet repose, I wonder if Nature herself is wondering if it should awaken on this morning. Is this quotidian event of the rising sun that we take for granted each morning a kind of miracle?

Am I a figure in a painting dreaming I am sitting in a garden in Fanjeaux, France?

Am I a person sitting in a garden in Fanjeaux, France dreaming I am a figure in a painting?

The boundaries between mind and nature are blurred as the "I" that I am seems to dissolve, as happened once before in the fields of Antarctic ice, and once before that in a hide in the bush of South Africa as the sun rose and the animals appeared at the water hole formed as if from the mist.

Before the word, before the thought, before the idea there is the gesture of a pointing finger in response to the opulence of the world's display. Children do it all the time and we, if we attend to the moment, understand that the pointing finger sketches out a path toward and into wonder.

In this place and in this moment thinking is dreaming!

So, as I give my arm and hand over to the world, I follow the arc of the finger toward the vast field of undulating hills that roll on toward the Black Mountains.

The hills are terraced and dotted with patches of brown earth, oases of green trees, nearby hilltop villages and the constant play of light and shadows as the sun wanders, stretching and spreading itself out almost shamelessly upon the land. The Black Mountains appear as a great high wave that has been building up as the hills roll toward it and at its apogee is just about to break upon the land. A play of tides! An erotic dance to the music of creation!

I can hear the music in the braying of a donkey that now and then sounds in the distance. Is it a cry of melancholy that this beauty of the natural world awakens? Do we share in some unknown way a bond of kinship as creatures that belong together to the earth? Is it in this great surround of nature that somehow his donkey world and mine come together?

The air as it glides through the trees tempts my nose with smells of summer fruit and caresses my skin with a touch as cool as blue water. The aroma of lavender rides the wind and I can hear the buzzing of bees as they go about their work that is a major mainstay of our food supply. The sensual flesh of my body vibrates in this erotic coupling with the sensuous flesh of the world. In this moment the world is holy and I suspect that our first responsive reply to the world is always a kind of prayer.

Time moves slowly and the relative silence becomes a doorway into the timeless sacred. A hint of eternity is cradled in the silence.

The melting polar ice

As Victor Frankenstein nears the end of telling his story to Captain Walton, the Monster that he created waits in the darkness of the cold Arctic night. After all the deaths that have happened in the wake of Victor's Promethean dream, only one thing remains for the Monster. As the Monster admits his own guilt for all that has happened, he seeks from Victor what his maker has never acknowledged, a small spark of awareness of his responsibility for the tragic consequences of his work. In their final encounter the Monster seeks a kind of blessing from his maker, some small sign of redemption, some few words from Frankenstein that would finally release him from his torment.

Looking upon his maker, he acknowledges that Victor Frankenstein is also his victim and he cries out:

> in his murder my crimes are consummated; the miserable series of my being is wound to its close! Oh, Frankenstein! generous and self devoted being! what does it avail that I now ask thee to pardon me?
>
> (Shelley, 1818)

But his maker is already dead and so there is no pardon bestowed upon him. For the last time he is now utterly abandoned and in the agony of this final loneliness, and in the presence of Captain Walton, who has been a witness throughout this final act, the Monster speaks these words that would seem to seal his fate:

> I shall quit your vessel on the ice raft that brought me hither, and shall seek
> the most northern extremity of the globe; I shall collect my funeral pile, and
> consume to ashes this miserable frame, that its remains may afford no light to
> any curious and unhallowed wretch, who would create such another as I have
> been. I shall die.
>
> *(Shelley, 1818)*

And so the story of Victor Frankenstein and his Monster winds back upon itself
toward its end. The light of the Promethean Mind that created him is now to be
extinguished in the frozen reaches of the Arctic night in the flames of the Monster's self-destruction.

> I shall ascend my funeral pile triumphantly, and exult in the agony of the
> torturing flames. The light of that conflagration will fade away; my ashes will
> be swept into the sea by the winds. My spirit will sleep in peace … Farewell.
>
> *(Shelley, 1818)*

With these words the Monster departs. Captain Walton, who is the last witness
of the Monster's presence, records the scene:

> He sprung from the cabin window, as he said this, upon the ice raft which lay
> close to the vessel. He was soon borne away by the waves, and lost in darkness
> and distance.
>
> *(Shelley, 1818)*

Mary Shelley's story ends here, but is it finished?
  Has the light faded away?
  Does the Monster's spirit sleep in peace?
  Is he now gone forever into darkness?
  Is the Monster dead?
  Is the fire still burning?

"We are such stuff as dreams are made on!"[8]

Victor Frankenstein's Prometheus Project is the stuff on which our collective
dreams are made, an economy so addicted to unlimited growth, whose global
appetite is so ravenous and insatiable, consuming the resources of nature at a rate
that seems monstrous, that it is now at odds with the finite limits of nature regarded as a resource for our use and abuse.

  In 2009, after I returned from a journey to the Antarctic, I made a DVD, *Antarctica: Inner Journeys in the Outer World.* [9] I was drawn to that place through a
dream that I had had thirty years earlier, a dream which I had forgotten but which
had not forgotten me. Drawn to that marginal landscape I met the Monster at the
end of the world. In that place, my dream found its source in Mary Shelley's

dream, Victor Frankenstein's dream and the Monster's dream as he crossed the threshold from death into life.

The Antarctic, a place of the heart as much as a location on a map, is a place where the awful beauty of the Monster shows its face. In that landscape of stillness and silence, of solitude and serenity, the intimate bond between mind and nature awakens the imagination, and from the depths of life a sorrow arises over the ways in which that bond is continuously and ever more ruthlessly being frayed. In that place its icy forms are like crystal cathedrals that house an ancient kind of prayer.

Antarctica: Inner Journeys in the Outer World and *The Frankenstein Prophecies* are home-comings, brief respites from the sense of not being so comfortably at home in the Promethean world.

Notes

1   When I use the phrase the dying of nature, I mean nature as we have constructed it as a technological world in which the natural world is taken to be a product of our own design. In this regard, every aspect of the natural world is treated as an object opposed to us as subjects, who as masters and lords of creation take on the role of the gods. In my earlier book, *Technology as Symptom and Dream* (1989/2006), I explored the cultural and historical origins of this subject as the spectator mind. For a description of this term and its appearance in this text see Question One, notes three and five, Question Six, note 12 and Question Eight, notes seven and eight.

While that book was a response in 1989 to the crisis of technological development, especially the threat of nuclear war, its scholarly approach was intended mainly for an academic audience. To my surprise it has had a long shelf life and is still in print. That fact has motivated me to take up the issue of technology again as the scope and speed of technological developments have spawned more dire crises, which now imperil the very existence of our world and us as well. If we are not quite yet on the list of endangered species, we are perilously close to joining that list.

As another response to these dangers, *The Frankenstein Prophecies* is a retelling of the origins of the spectator mind, which is intended now for the wider audience of all who are now becoming increasingly aware of the dangers, for each of us who, daily confronted with the seemingly endless display of disturbing news, are overwhelmed and even at times benumbed by forecasts of a dreaded fate.

Using Mary Shelley's story, the character of Victor Frankenstein, whose dream of becoming a new god capable of bestowing life, is the dramatic personification of the spectator mind. One of the prophetic consequences of his dream explored in *The Frankenstein Prophecies* is how his imposition of his view of nature as merely a resource for his work haunts us today as the dying of that way of framing nature as a technological matter. As such, the natural world becomes a mirror that reflects an image of who we are as masters of creation. That face is the visage of the Monster, the other side of Victor Frankenstein's god face, as it were, the delusional face of the dream to act as if we are gods. If we now turn away from that image, we are turning away from the path that might transform what seems to be a fate into a prophecy that questions and challenges us into another way of being responsive to the dangers of technology. The intention of *The Frankenstein Prophecies* is to open a way between an unquestioning embrace of technological developments and a Luddite rejection of it.

While this distinction between saying nature is dying and nature as we have framed it as a technological matter is dying is essential, I will leave the title of Question Two as it is and clarify its use in the text with the felicitous phrase, "nature as we know it," suggested by a reviewer of the manuscript.

I would add here that this distinction between saying nature is dying and nature as we know it is dying is part of the fabric of Martin Heidegger's philosophy. It is also a philosophical basis of the work I have done over the years regarding technology. For some important texts about Heidegger's reflections on technology, see the following: Rojcewicz (2006); Sheehan (2015); Mugerauer (2008); Sipiora (1991).

2   The moon, the making of the Monster's mate and the destruction of that mate appear throughout the manuscript because they are some of the archetypal patterns and mythical motifs threaded throughout Mary Shelley's work. These three threads alongside, for example, Victor Frankenstein as a modern Prometheus and the Monster as an emblem of the shadow that haunts Victor Frankenstein's dream and work comprise the fabric of Shelley's story as prophecy. Their recurrence draws out how each of these motifs underlies the specific theme of a particular question. Their appearances are context dependent. In addition, their various contexts display the interconnection among all the motifs.

I have written my book intentionally not so much as a linear argument designed to make a logical case. Rather, I have written it as if the story I am telling unwinds as a spiral in which essential patterns and motifs return at a different level, reminding readers of what has already been said while alerting them to what is coming again in a strange but familiar way. It is a rhetorical style where repetition is used to bring attention to a central theme.

This style uncovers and reveals the concealed links among cultural and historical events and the archetypal patterns that connect them. One of these patterns is the Monster's tale and his haunting presence in the crises we explore in the first six questions. In this regard, *The Frankenstein Prophecies* is a shadow history that is not a chronological history of shadows. This shadow history attends to the lingering presence of unconscious dynamics in the ways in which we understand the past and write its history. It was an approach I used in *Technology as Symptom and Dream.*

It is also an approach that the historian Norman Cohn advised in the postscript of his book, *Europe's Inner Demons.* Exploring the European history of witches, he affirms he was investigating "above all a fantasy at work in history" and that "It is fantasy, and nothing else that provides the continuity in this story." And while his study of this fantasy makes use of all the tools of the historian's craft, he confesses at the end of his postscript the need to attend to the "depths, which were not to be explored by the techniques at my disposal." Others, he says, are needed "to venture further downwards, into the abyss of the unconscious" (1977, p. 258).

The Frankenstein Prophecies explores this abyss in moving toward the Monster on the margins of Victor Frankenstein's fantasy of becoming a new creator god.

I would add here my debt to my mentor, J. H. van den Berg, whose approach to psychology was through culture and history. He called his approach metabletics to indicate the changing character of human understanding and the co-constructed nature of reality. In 2008 I edited a special edition of his work, which is a good introduction to his life and work. See Janus Head (2008).

3   I use a capital letter for She to underscore two key points of *The Frankenstein Prophecies.* First, She is the excluded feminine that haunts the shadows of Victor's Spectator Mind. Second, like the Monster, She lives on in the many guises of her prophetic descendants. Some of those disguises are discussed later.

While many writers have addressed this issue of Mary Shelley's story from the critical perspective of feminism, I take up this aspect from the archetypal point of view of Jung's psychology. The two approaches do not contradict each other. They complement each other. For an example of a feminist perspective within a cultural context, see Susan Tyler Hitchcock, *Frankenstein: A Cultural History* (2007).

4   The triad of Prometheus, his brother Epimetheus and Pandora, the wife of Epimetheus, offers an insightful perspective on the question regarding the dead woman as the price for Victor's Promethean dream.

In the myth, Prometheus, whose name means forethought or foresight, is the creator of mankind, but dissatisfied with the lot imposed upon them by the gods, he steals fire from the gods and gives it to mankind. Angered by this action, the gods take their revenge through Epimetheus, whose name means afterthought or hindsight. Prometheus has warned his brother against taking any gifts from the gods, and especially warns him not to take Pandora, whose name means the "all-giver," as his bride. But, of course, as in so many mythic tales about the gods and humans, the warning is the very thing that sets the course of the story.

So Epimetheus does take Pandora as his bride, and when she opens the jar that was given to her as a wedding gift from Zeus, she releases all the evils upon humankind. But there is one gift that remains in the jar. It is the gift of hope to ease the sufferings of humankind.

We could conclude that Pandora spoils Prometheus's work of creation and then draw a parallel with Victor Frankenstein, as the modern Prometheus. Foreseeing that Elizabeth Lavenza was too naïve and lacked the kind of rigor of mind needed for his work, he excludes her from the very beginning of it. And, when in his second act of creation he realizes the horror of what he has done, he destroys the mate he promised to his Monster. But if we stop here, then we leave out that Pandora's jar still has the seed of hope. In his discussion of the myth of Prometheus, Ivan Illich has appealed to us to remember the place of Epimetheus and Pandora in the story. Linking the Promethean tale to the consumer ethos that is exhausting the earth, he writes: "We need a name for those who love the earth on which each can meet the other. We need a name for those who collaborate with their Promethean brother in the lighting of the fire" (Illich, 1970, pp. 115–116).

For Illich that name is Epimetheus. To make a place for Epimetheus in the tale of Prometheus, is to re-imagine the feminine figure of Pandora who bears the gift of hope. If the feminine presence in the guises of Pandora, Eve, Elizabeth Lavenza and the Monster's mate are sidelined, exiled, marginalized as spoilers of creation, then so too is hope, as the gift that allows one to endure in the face of evil and all its tragedies. The seed of hope that remains in Pandora's jar is born in the tension between the Promethean will that in leaping ahead is able to imagine what might be and the Epimethean pause to remember what the consequences of that leap have been. Between imagination and memory human kind carries the fragile vessel of hope.

That jar breaks when the forethought of imagination, with all its wondrous and exciting appeals, leaps ahead without memory of what is being changed. The figure and story of Victor Frankenstein exemplifies the destructive character of this unchecked Promethean imagination.

That jar also breaks when the afterthought or hindsight of memory becomes a nostalgic longing for and destructive repetition of some past age. The rise of political nationalism in Germany in the 1930s and its apparent repetition today in the USA are good examples. The tale of Prometheus, Epimetheus and Pandora is an exemplary warning. Is not the story of Victor Frankenstein as the modern Prometheus a similar warning?

For another comment on Prometheus, see Glen Slater (1997). He points out that Prometheus bound is where we are called to listen to what is addressing us from beyond the borders of mind. This point is central to *The Frankenstein Prophecies*. Attending to the Monster's tale, we are addressed from the margins of Victor Frankenstein's Promethean mind.

5   Just as Eve stands for an archetypal dimension in the human psyche, I use a capital letter for Woman to make the same point. See note three above.

6   See for example Carolyn Merchant's classic text *The Death of Nature: Women, Ecology and the Scientific Revolution* (1983). Moreover, while developments in twentieth century physics, biology and chemistry, for example, have gone well beyond this paradigm, much of our technology has its roots in it, as witnessed by the ongoing destruction of vast areas of nature.

7   For an excellent discussion of this theme see Naomi Klein, *This Changes Everything* (2014).

8   This line is from Shakespeare's *The Tempest*. For detailed information see Question Seven, note six.

9   See http://robertromanyshyn.jigsy.com/.

Question Three

THE MONSTER'S BODY

Is Mary Shelley's story a prophecy of the Monster's descendants?

The complexities of love

The most miserable of creatures, alone and shunned by all, made malicious, as he acknowledges to his maker, by his suffering, his vices the consequence of his forced exile beyond the human community, he seeks nothing from his creator except a mate of the same species as himself, a bride who, disfigured as he is, would not shrink in horror and disgust from him, a companion in isolation with whom he would retreat to the most remote regions of the world where neither his maker nor any other human being would ever see them again, and where he and his bride might in their own way become happy.

> I swear to you, by the earth which I inhabit, and by you that made me, that, with the companion you bestow, I will quit the neighbourhood of man, and dwell, as it may chance, in the most savage of places.
>
> *(Shelley, 1818)*

This is the Monster's promise to Victor Frankenstein. Even in the most isolated places, even on the margins of the human community, the love of another will temper the Monster's loneliness, make it bearable, and bestow some measure of happiness. The love of another, he says to his maker, will even extinguish the reason for his crimes:

> If I have no ties and no affections, hatred and vice must be my portion; the love of another will destroy the cause of my crimes ... My vices are the children of a forced solitude that I abhor; and my virtues will necessarily arise when I live in communion with an equal. I shall feel the affections of a

sensitive being, and become linked to the chain of existence and events, from which I am now excluded.

(Shelley, 1818)

Sworn before Victor Frankenstein, his maker and his god, the Monster's promise is an oath that affirms the redemptive power of love. His words are perhaps even a prayer that intimates that beneath all the violence, death and destruction Mary Shelley's story is a tangled love story. In the tension between Victor Frankenstein and the Monster, her story dramatically portrays how monsters are made in the complexities of love, especially when love is masked as power.

Victor Frankenstein, who has continuously turned a deaf ear to the Monster's appeals, is finally moved by his eloquent pleas, which stir in him a glimmer of recognition of his obligation to the Monster he made. Extracting from the Monster his promise to quit Europe forever, and every other place in the neighborhood of man, Victor agrees to a second creation. He will do what he has done before; he will make a mate for the Monster.

Would Mary Shelley's story be remembered today if Victor kept his promise? Would her story shine brightly today as a beacon of hope when we do take responsibility for our actions, rather than as a prophecy regarding the lethal and destructive consequences of denial?

It would not because it is the conflict between Victor and the Monster that gives her story its tragic plot.[1] Their struggle underscores how the webs of power and love and one's obligations to others and the denial of those obligations entrap both of them in the dramas of death and destruction. So Victor must renege on his promise and the Monster must exact his revenge. This story, told and retold many times, has haunted the collective imagination because it portrays the enormous difficulties of learning how to love in the shadow of death. Shelley's story depicts how human love might be, as the Poet Rilke has said, the most difficult work of all.[2]

As he works to create a mate for his Monster, the shock at what he is doing reminds him that the enthusiasm with which he worked to make his creature is now crippled with doubt and a sense of foreboding. Might one of the first fruits of the love that would bind the two together, he wonders, be children and beyond that a race of devils that would fill the earth and imperil the very existence of the species of man?

Consumed by his doubt and foreboding, Victor's sense of obligation to his Monster weakens. As it does, the full horror of what he has done takes hold of him, and when, in the light of the moon, he sees the mate he promised to create for his Monster, he shudders as he imagines that future ages will curse him as one who bought his own peace of mind at the price of endangering the whole human race. In rage and fury and fear he tears her asunder as the Monster watches.

This is one of those threshold moments in the story when Victor and the Monster have crossed a boundary from which there is no return. In his destructive act, Frankenstein believes he has sacrificed himself for the benefit of the human race. Now no children will be born of his god like dream to create life. With this brutal act Victor assures himself that the Monster will have no descendants. And, as he watches Victor destroy his last bit of hope to be bonded in love with another, the Monster, who was the first of his kind, fears he is condemned to be the last of his kind.

But is Frankenstein's Monster the last of his kind?

Are no descendants born in the wreckage of this tangled tale of love corrupted by power, of hope betrayed by despair, of responsibilities and obligations that are denied?

Or, are we the prophetic offspring of the Monster, the ones that Victor Frankenstein feared, the Monster's descendants, the shadow children of Victor Frankenstein's omnipotent dream?

The blueprint for the Monster's body

When Victor Frankenstein begins his work, he draws upon the established tradition of medical training. The origins of that tradition were laid almost three hundred years earlier in 1543 when Andreas Vesalius published *On the Fabric of the Human Body*, which is credited with being the first modern textbook in anatomy. It was a daring work that overthrew the authority of the Roman physician Galen, which had lasted for more than a thousand years, and challenged the Catholic Church's ban on dissecting the dead human body.

Prior to Vesalius a physician would read from the works of Galen as a lowly barber surgeon cut into the flesh. Vesalius did his own bloody work. Cutting into the body, he illustrated with careful and detailed drawings what his dissections revealed. Knife in hand he did not just penetrate the boundary of flesh to lay open the interior cavities of the body. With the first cut he also profaned the Church's view of the sacred quality of the human body. With the first drops of blood that still might ooze from the dissected flesh, the dead human body, which at the end of time was to be resurrected into its final judgment of heaven or hell, would begin to disappear. At the edge of the skin, the dead human body was being changed into an anatomical corpse.

Of all the illustrations in his text, the one of Vesalius himself most displays this change.[3] Looking directly at the reader, his pose is confident as he holds the right arm of a dead body. The skin has been flayed away to reveal the muscles inside the arm, but it is now an arm that belongs to no one, or to anyone or to everyone. The flayed arm is a part of the body seen as a specimen. It is an anonymous body created by Vesalius's anatomical gaze.

Victor Frankenstein's spectator mind looks at the body in the same way and it is the specimen body whose processes of decay and decomposition he observes in the charnel houses he visits and the specimen bodies he digs up in those churchyard cemeteries.

Frankenstein as Prophecy

The first of his kind but not the last, Victor Frankenstein's Monster is a kind of being who continues to face us with questions about what constitutes being a human being. In his specimen body, which is the blueprint for Victor Frankenstein's work, the Monster is a paradox. On one hand, his body, as an assemblage of anatomical parts, is an object, a thing. On the other hand, his bodily actions show him to be an independent subject with intention, purpose and direction. The context of a medical examination reminds us that we are this strange paradox.

The medical body

The specimen body is the body observed, the body that Vesalius creates as an object of his anatomical gaze. It is the foundation of the medical body, the body that is the focus of the medical examination. It is the objective body that one has compared with the subjective body that one is, the body as a thing in space compared with the body as one's standpoint in the world whose movements transform space into places of meaningful actions, into a stage where the dramas of a person's life are enacted. What is remarkable about the human body is that these comparisons are not dualisms. On the contrary, the human body can present itself as an object because it is more than an object. The unique character of the human body is that the body one is effortlessly slides into the body one has and vice versa.[4]

In the context of the medical examination, the body one has is handed over, as it were, to the physician. With a hand surgeon, for example, the person's hand that shakes the doctor's hand is not the same as the anatomical hand that the physician X-rays, and no X-ray will reveal to the physician that the bones and joints he sees are those of Mr. A who is a pianist. The same paradox applies to the physician. For example, the hand of a proctologist or gynecologist that examines a man's prostate or a women's womb is not the same as the hand that greets the patient. In each of these medical contexts, the physician's hand is impersonal. It is a doctor's hand, a skilled instrument, as it were. It is not the hand of the specific person who is the doctor.

The medical exam is a special situation where the paradoxical character of the human body appears. In this situation, a person is able to lend the body he or she *has* to a physician because he or she *is* a body. In the medical context, one is able to lend his or her body as an object to be examined because he or she is not an object.

But the specimen body also displays itself in the midst of our daily lives. Washing one's hands is a direct and simple example of this paradoxical nature of the human body. In every moment of washing one's hands, there is a continuous interchange between the washing hand and the hand that is washed. It is so subtle a crossing between the two that it takes a concerted effort to remain focused on either the hand that is doing the washing or the hand that is being washed. One has to step back from the action, remove oneself from the situation and look upon it from a distance as if one were a spectator. But even with the most attentive effort one cannot sustain one's focus because each hand slides between being washed and doing the washing. The spectator you try to be is pulled down and into the living situation.

Without usually realizing it, we attest to this remarkable and unique character of the human body in our language. When I say, for example, "I am washing myself," I am using a reflexive verb to describe this simple everyday wonder in which a washing hand reflects, or bends back upon, or folds into a hand that is washed. The statement also refers to the active and passive forms of verbs. "Myself" is the receiver of the action that "I" actively do.

But this ordinary wonder ordinarily goes down the drain. The consequence of this ordinary wonder ordinarily slipping away is that the specimen body becomes the norm of what we take to be the true reality of the body.[5] For example, the specimen body has become a commodity within the very profitable nexus of the medical, pharmaceutical and insurance industries. In this tangled web, the crises that surround the costs of health care and the overuse of medical drugs that lead, for example, to opioid addiction, illustrate that side of the Monster's specimen body that served as the blueprint for Frankenstein's dream. In an ironic twist of his fate, the Monster who swore that he and his mate would quit the neighborhood of humanity forever has been dragged into the market place. We might wonder if he and his mate have also become commodities for the pornographic industry where the body as object is on display.

Victor Frankenstein's Monster *is* and *is not* this specimen body and within this paradox we are like him. In this Question Three we follow two lines of his descendants that arise from this paradox that live on today as the Monster's progeny, which Victor Frankenstein so feared.

On one hand, this line of descendants perfects the body that Victor Frankenstein created but abandoned because of the Monster's horrible imperfections. With genetic manipulation and computer generated images we are not only erasing the ageing process that promises the illusion of being forever young, these technologies are also creating bodies that experiment with making an ideal human body.

On the other hand, there is a line of descendants that haunts the margins of these dreams of a perfect, ageless and ideal human body. Like the Monster, these descendants live in exile, shunned by and invisible to those who are perfected.

These two lines of descent branch off from each other in the gap between the blink and the wink.

In the blink of an eye

The body observed is not the observing body. The eye that sees the eye as an anatomical object is more than the site where the physics of light and the physiology of that eye converge. The eye that sees the eye in that way is an insight into a way of imagining sight.

There is more to seeing than meets the eyeball. The eye that is said to be the window of the soul is not the anatomical eye that blinks. The blinking eye is a reflex, a physiological mechanism that serves a biological function. It is also a reflex that can be made responsive to cultural conditioning. But again the conditioned eye is not the same as the eye that envisions this possibility.

The eye that winks at the other is not the blinking eye. A winking eye is a coded message; it carries a meaning. To glance at you and nod in passing is not the same as to glare at you in anger. To gaze lovingly into the eyes of one's beloved is not to ogle or leer or even stare at her or him. The glance, the glare, the gaze and the stare, the leer or the look that ogles the other are distinctly different ways of embodying vision. Each act is qualitatively different from the others, and no ophthalmological device can take the measure of that difference. Nor can any such device measure the difference between the creative eye of the painter and the biological eye of the ophthalmologist. In like manner, voyeurism is not an ophthalmological problem. It is a style of action, problematic to be sure, but one for which an eye exam and a new pair of glasses is no solution.

The eye that winks is an animated eye, the eye that is the power to take up the biological and cultural conditions of behavior and turn them into styles of action in the world. In this difference that seems so insignificant a quantum leap is made. Between the blink and the wink a gap is crossed when one interrupts for a moment an automatic process and transforms mechanism into meaning, instinct into an intentional act. Leaping across that gap is what makes us more than a specimen body. It is what makes us human. Try as one might, and as much as one might love his or her dog, the dog blinks and might even be conditioned to wink, but that wink will never be one that jumps the gap into an intentional and meaningful act. In that leap a human being emerges as one who creatively can imagine the possibility of possibility.

But what about Victor Frankenstein's Monster?

Made of multiple parts from the remains of buried corpses and then sparked into life, does he take up the conditions of his creation and transform them into a way of being in the world?

Is he human?

Does he wink?

While there is no incident in Mary Shelley's story where he winks, we know that he has that human capacity to do so. We know it because when she describes the dream from which Victor and his Monster are born, she says that at the moment when the Monster awakens Victor from sleep and is standing at his maker's bedside, he looks upon Victor with speculative eyes. The anatomical eye does not convey wonder at what it sees; it does not convey curiosity; it does not speculate about these or other possibilities.[6]

But those eyes that do look upon his maker with speculation and wonder are what make Mary Shelley's story more than a supernatural horror story. Those questioning eyes shape her story as a human drama. It is one of many moments that testify to the Monster's ability to take a stand against the conditions of his creation, one occasion of the Monster's assertive resistance against his creator god. The Monster's speculative eyes are a testament to his capacity to transform the conditions of his birth into *his* story. Although he understands himself as the new Adam, unlike his biblical counterpart he is not simply thrown out of Paradise. On the contrary, he chooses his fate. Throughout the story his actions assert his resistance to and rebellion against his maker's image of a scientifically planned and technologically engineered paradise. The Monster asserts that he was not made for that paradise.[7]

Victor Frankenstein's Monster is a curious and puzzling creature. The Monster's body does not matter only as matter, as only raw material for Victor's work.

Though monstrous in his form, he is not a mere caricature of a human being. He is not a mere puppet whose strings are pulled by his master. His form does not just mimic that of a human being. Although hideous in his disfigurement, he still matters. In spite of his grotesque and shocking features, we recognize a kinship with him. He is still like us, a being, for example, whose heart, like ours, is more than a pumping mechanism, whose loneliness, like ours, is heartfelt.

His kinship with us is what makes Mary Shelley's story so important today. The Monster takes us to the boundaries and edges of the question of what makes a human being different from a machine or a robot. His presence forces upon us the question of what constitutes personhood.[8] In his likeness to us we understand his suffering. Below the surface of mind, before any judgment is made, we are touched and moved by his plight. It is difficult to turn away. Our kinship with him is an emotional bond and this bond, as tenuous as we might want it to be with the Monster, is what makes Mary Shelley's story so poignant and sad.

Monsters on the margins

When Victor Frankenstein agrees to make a mate for the Monster, it is on the condition that the Monster and his mate will seek out places most distant from any human community. Such a promise was possible at that time, but since then the world has been so planned and charted, so wired into the World Wide Web and its Google maps, that no such isolated places exist. The Monster's progeny, born from his maker's dream to be a new god, and from his maker's abandonment of him and his subsequent exile, isolation and loneliness, have had to find other places.

Where are they?

Who are they?

A voice from the shadows

Recently while walking in the SOHO district of New York with some members of my family, I was stopped by the voice of a woman who was sitting in the shadows of a building. It was twilight and it was getting colder. In a voice that had a haunting almost oracular quality to it, she was saying over and over again, "What is the matter with you people? Don't you see what is happening?" It was as if a spell was cast over me by her words and the quality of her appeal. I went over to her and asked if she needed help. A story tumbled forth from her about poverty and illness of herself, her daughter and her grandchildren. But even as she was telling her story, I could see she was not telling it to me, not even looking at me. Her gaze carried her words into the world that surrounded us. The tragedy and sorrow of this encounter was that she was invisible to those who were rushing past her.

The homeless person on the streets of our major cities, the bag lady pushing her shopping cart, the broken man poking in garbage cans for scraps of food, the wounded war veteran by the side of the road with his or her sign asking for help, the jobless person whose sign says he or she will work for food, linger in their isolation and loneliness on the margins of our world. We hurry by and as we do we want to assure ourselves that they are not like us and we are certainly not like them.

They are disposable people, the throw away people, the figures and faces who mirror what seems alien and monstrous to us.

But if the progeny of Victor's Monster are, like the Monster himself, like us, then what are the consequences of a denial, which, in exiling them to the marginal outposts of our world, would make them less human than us?

How is our own humanity endangered if we deny the personhood of these descendants of the Monster, like we do with the Monster himself?

What happens to our own humanity if we forget our kinship with the Monster and his kin?

Maybe Mary Shelley's story is a horror story, because it does present these questions when and if we linger with the Monster on the margins of her story where, making a place for the Monster's tale, we are addressed by these questions. Perhaps that is also why the Monster has generally appeared in a bad light in the many variations of her story.

Disturbing as they are, these questions have become more insistent as the homeless and jobless, the bag ladies and men picking scraps from garbage cans, the war veterans and the swelling army of dispensable others in so many other guises are becoming more visible. But even while this is happening, the other line of descendants of Victor Frankenstein and his Monster are appearing in another place not only quite different from the margins, but also much less, if at all, disturbing.

Consumers in shopping malls[9]

Shopping malls might be seen as the last place, and the most unexpected place, to find descendants of the Monster. They are, after all, ubiquitous and convenient, for they contain all kinds of stores to satisfy almost any need. There are fast food restaurants for anyone who wants a quick meal as well as more upscale dining places at least in some malls, where one might meet friends for a more leisurely lunch or dinner. There are shops for clothes and furniture, boutiques for elegant and special items, hardware stores and home improvement outlets for the serious and weekend handy man and woman, flower shops and candy places, jewelry stores and even banks and numerous cash machines to get the money to buy all that stuff that one wants. For the tasty snack, there are coffee shops and bakeries whose aromas tempt even the less than hungry. There are also movie metroplexes with multiple films and all day showings. All of that washed in bright and shiny hues with programmed music, the elevator music to soothe the ups and downs of life, pervading it all.

For Victor Frankenstein, the blueprint of the specimen body gave him the raw material for his god like dream to create life. Shopping malls are temples to the god of matter where progeny of the Monster's specimen body can be at home.

Specifically designed for happiness, malls are places where one might, at least for a while, escape the worries and sorrows, the boredom and the loneliness of one's life. They are places where one expects to be able to pack up his or her troubles and chase all his or her cares away. In an ironic twist of Victor's demand that his Monster and his mate had to seek out the farthest places beyond the reach of humanity, shopping malls are that place. In the guise of the consumer, shopping malls are where descendants of the Monster's specimen body shamble along with packages in hand.

It is a very long way from the bag lady or the homeless man on the street, from the wounded war veteran or the out of work, hungry job seeker to the shopping mall. Trying to find one's way, it is easy to get lost and to forget that margins and malls are connected. While malls do not fulfill Victor Frankenstein's dream of defeating the Great Spoiler Death, their delight is a consumer's heaven where death can for a while be denied.[10] Is it not then so much more preferable to linger in the malls than on the margins where the Monster's progeny can spoil our tranquility?

The Botox face

Smoothing out the lines and wrinkles of the face, firming up sagging jowls and necklines, the Botoxed face erases these marks of ageing, corruption and decay. Offering the promise of being young again, and maybe perpetually so, the Botox face conceals the marks of time, the cuts that time itself carves into the flesh. An offspring of Victor's Monster, the Botoxed face can avoid the loneliness that the Monster's hideous scars enforced upon him. But as it does so something seems lost, for the surgically remade face erases more than the marks of ageing. It also erases how these marks etched by time show the character of the person, the life that has been lived. With that loss, moreover, something of the beauty of the human face also seems sacrificed. The old man on a park bench smoking a pipe in a cool autumn morning may show the passerby the arc of his life with its own peculiar terrible kind of beauty that makes one pause for a moment in recognition of one's own life as it moves inevitably toward its own resting place. Dolls have smooth faces, people do not! What happens to us if we begin to live among dolls?

The plastic surgeon's office offers a detour away from the Monster's kin on the margins, where the bag lady or the homeless person have to face their situation, toward the kin of Frankenstein who continue his dream toward the eventual eradication of death. Indeed, the Botox face along with all the other surgically manipulated possibilities from breast implants and penile enlargement to the transhumanist speculations about creating new bodies via surgical and computer technologies are visions of the perfect body, which are inching increasingly closer toward Frankenstein's dream.[11]

The idea of perfection, however, is an unreal ideal in human life, and its use as a measure has harsh consequences, as Victor Frankenstein's own words show:

> It was already one in the morning; the rain pattered dismally against the panes, and my candle was nearly burnt out, when by the glimmer of the half-extinguished light, I saw the dull yellow eye of the creature open … His limbs were in proportion, and I had selected his features as beautiful. Beautiful!—

Great God! His yellow skin scarcely covered the work of muscles and arteries beneath; his hair was of a lustrous black, and flowing; his teeth of a pearly whiteness; but these luxuriances only formed a more horrid contrast with his watery eyes, that seemed almost of the same colour as the dun white sockets in which they were set, his shrivelled complexion, and straight black lips ... the beauty of the dream vanished, and breathless horror and disgust filled my heart. Unable to endure the aspect of the being I had created, I rushed out of my room.

(Shelley, 1818)

As Victor Frankenstein's kin and kind carry forward his dream, they might also draw back in horror and disgust from those less than perfect specimens on the margins.[12]

The camera eye of the consumer

Shopping malls are spectacles of display and the detours to them from the margins offer multiple spectacles to delight and dazzle the spectator mind of the consumer. Indeed, the world itself has become a spectacle of display to be observed and recorded for our use and pleasure. What better instrument than the camera for the specimen eye of the consumer, since the camera itself is modeled on that anatomical eye?

When George Romero was making *Dawn of the Dead*, his 1978 sequel to his first Zombie film, *Night of the Living Dead* made ten years earlier, he chose a mall for its setting. That choice was made, he said, because he noticed the blissful state of the consumers as they walked through the mall. In that moment a connection was made between consumer and Zombie like behavior. Romero's Zombie films have become a cult classic that have pervaded the collective imagination, as the success of the television series, *The Walking Dead*, indicates.

Victor's Monster is not a Zombie. Zombies, the dark twin of the consumer, are one line of the Monster's offspring, progeny that Victor Frankenstein wanted to prevent.

In the form of Zombies, the specimen body turns upon itself as the raw material of the specimen body becomes the object of consumption for insatiable appetites. The consumer body with its voracious appetites for stuff mimics that behavior. Greed for material things becomes a new good and the mantra shop till you drop caricatures the purposeless walk of the Zombies. The consumer body, lulled by the vapid sounds of piped in music, moves forward in a kind of bliss filled numb stupor.

The shopping mall setting in Romero's film has become part of the world programmed for tourism. The Zombie shuffle can be seen almost everywhere now, as tourists with cameras in hand gobble up the scenery. The consumer mind feeds on the landscapes scheduled along the way. Click by click the digital image captured by the spectator eye replaces the experience of the place. Memories that were carried in the heart to be told later as stories that reimagine and reanimate the experience become images to look at of a world that has become a spectacle to be seen. Pilgrimage, the art of wandering in wonder in landscapes both sacred and secular, has become the guided tour.

Outside *The Museu Nacional d'Art de Catalunya* in Barcelona, a wandering troop of tourists are purchasing selfie-sticks. With them in hand the camera eye of the consumer extends the range of its vision and captures with the despotic eye of the spectator mind the self that can even include itself in the spectacle.

What happens to the capacity to be lost when paths are measured and mapped?

What happens to the capacity to be surprised when paths are clocked and timed?

What happens to places of beauty and wonder, like the beautiful architecture of *The Museu Nacional d'Art de Catalunya*, when they are photographed and digitalized to show—show off—one was there?

Tourism might be a kind of terrorism.[13]

A flawed god

The offspring of Victor Frankenstein and the Monster who is immediately disowned by his maker are telling their tales in these disguised forms of consumers in shopping malls, tourists with their camera eyes, Botoxed bodies, bag people and war veterans, and the countless homeless people who haunt the marginal spaces of our overly sanitized world. These kin and kind of Victor Frankenstein's god like dream are some of the prophetic streams that flow from Mary Shelley's story.

As such they are like canaries in the coalmine warning us that we make monsters and make them invisible when either we deny responsibility for what we have made, or become oblivious to their presence.

This denial is a slippery slope toward justifying violence against all that is judged as Other, as evil, as demon or devil as Victor labels his Monster.

This denial is a slippery slope that allows us not to see how our economic and political policies create the homeless person on the street, the bag lady or man poking in garbage cans for a scrap of food, the wounded war veteran by the side of the road with a cardboard crayoned sign asking for help, or at least some recognition that he or she is not invisible.

Denial is also the means that makes us more invisible to ourselves, the means by which we relieve ourselves of responsibility for the actions we have taken and the things we have created.

Mary Shelley's story is a primer of human kind acting as if we are gods and denying responsibility for the consequences of our actions. It is a classic text about the dangers of being a false god.[14]

Notes

1 For this difference between story and plot see E. M. Forster's (1980) *Aspects of the Novel*.

2 See Rilke (1934), *Letters to a Young Poet*.

3 A detailed description of the work of Vesalius and its impact on changing the view of the human body in Western culture is in my book, *Technology as Symptom and Dream* (Romanyshyn, 1989/2006). The illustration of Vesalius is Figure 4.7.

   See also Question One, note three.

4 Phenomenology offers many detailed works on this paradoxical character of the human body. The work of Maurice Merleau-Ponty (1942/1963, 1945/1962 and 1968) is especially important. For an overview of his work see Romanyshyn (2011).

5 Tongue in cheek here, we might say that Descartes's dualism between the mind that thinks and the body as a thing that one might think about makes him into a plumber's philosopher. I actually met a plumber once who said this to me. But it was in our house in France and so it made sense to me. I even wondered for a moment if he carried in his toolbox a copy of Descartes's *Meditations*.

6 Descartes (1637/1971) says in *The Dioptrics* that in order to understand how the eye works one must use the eye of a newly dead man. This is the material that Victor Frankenstein uses for the creation of his monster. In his work the dead would live again, and the blind would see. While we have not yet arrived at that place where the dead can be resurrected, that possibility is certainly being explored in the fields of genetics and computer technologies. We will explore this issue in Questions Four and Five. But, through advances made in understanding the anatomical and physiological process of vision we are able in some instances to restore a kind of sight to the blind. There are things about Victor Frankenstein's dream to be appreciated. Even the simple act of wearing eye-glasses displays the advantages that follow on our increasing knowledge of the specimen body. Indeed, it might help our discussion of this line of descendants to imagine Victor's Monster wearing eye-glasses. Such an image not only humanizes the Monster, it also awakens us to how he is like us in the paradoxical nature of his embodiment.

7 Are we made for Paradise? Is the technologically made world the Paradise we imagined? Or does it at times feel more like Hell? In many ways Victor's Monster as a tragic character mirrors how the image of paradise, whether in the Christian religious creation story or the modern scientific-technological creation story, is an illusion spawned by the fear and denial of death. Moreover, that the Monster educates himself by reading John Milton's *Paradise Lost* alerts us to the possibility that the Monster, as the shadow of Victor Frankenstein's god image of himself, plays the same role as does Lucifer in Milton's epic. In both creation stories, the Monster as Devil and the Devil as monster are figures who warn us we are not made for paradise. In this context see the work of the Romanian philosopher Emil Cioran, especially *The Trouble with Being Born* (1973).

8 This question is at the heart of the abortion debate, as noted in Question One.

9 On Monday November 27, 2017, I was working on *The Frankenstein Prophecies* in a coffee shop in NOLA when a reporter and a camera man were filming a news story about this day being Cyber Monday. When I asked them if they were interested in a counter view to this digital excess of consumerism, they said they were but could not sell it to their editor even though they agreed with my remarks regarding on line living and shopping and the erosion of community, place and so on. What has happened to the sacred quality of Thanksgiving when it is followed by Black Friday and now Cyber Monday?

10 Mall shootings suggest the death denied is also erupting there.

11 Transhumanism is a logical extension of Victor Frankenstein's work. One significant difference is the focus of transhumanism on the perfectibility of the human body through the application of our increasing genetic capabilities coupled with computer technology. In this context, the place of death in human life gives way to the unquestioned belief in our capacities to go beyond the limits of natural evolution and directing its course. We will meet an exponent of this belief in Question Five where the work of Ray Kurzweil is discussed in some detail. For the moment, I would point out that while a primary argument in favor of transhumanism is its application to disease, there is also the argument that frames its images as an aesthetic argument that covers over the ethical dimension of this work. Perfectibility here is in service to overcoming the marks of ageing in the pursuit of beauty. As we have seen perfection and beauty were ideals that shaped Victor Frankenstein's creation of his Monster.

12 I had a recent example of this behavior in Jackson Square in New Orleans. In addition to the many artists and tarot car readers offering their wares, the square was filled with

tourists, who passed by the numerous homeless people sitting or sleeping on the benches. They were invisible to the tourists and it seemed to me they were unaware of their kinship: tourists and the homeless as inverse descendants of the Monster!

13 I am not diminishing the difference between violent acts of terrorism and tourism. It is a difference with an essential distinction. My suggestion is an analogy that recently was brought home to me in Collioure in France where my wife and I were exploring the regions where the light was a key factor that inspired Mattisse and André Derain to create Fauvism in 1905. Lingering in the light, dreaming of those two painters wandering the coastal harbors and streets, my reverie was interrupted by a group of tourists who were walking behind the group leader who was carrying a yellow flag. What struck me was the dutiful style of the group and the look on their faces, which were focused straight ahead. There was a mood of emptiness about them that made them look robotic, as if they were Zombies waiting to feast on the next sight along the tour. They were present in that space for that moment in time, but they were not in the place of Collioure with Matisse and Derain in 1905. Tourism is the manifestation of what we become when neutral spaces have supplanted places with character, and time as a line has supplanted the layered and cyclical depths of time within which Matisse and Derain are still painting.

14 *Sapiens: A Brief History of Humankind* (2011) by Yuval Noah Harari is an inspiring tale of the evolution of our species that challenges us to consider where we are today and where we are going. In the "Afterword: The Animal that Became a God," he ends his book with this most significant question: "Is there anything more dangerous than dissatisfied and irresponsible gods who don't know what they want?" *The Frankenstein Prophecies* not only shares this question, it also presents Victor Frankenstein as a prophetic emblem of that most dangerous god. *Homo Deus* (2017), Harari's follow up to *Sapiens*, is his reply.

While I acknowledge the critical importance of Harari's two books for the way in which they present a sober and careful context for a future that is rapidly approaching us, I find *Homo Deus* to be a flawed reply to his question because he misunderstands the crucial dimension of how unconscious dynamics shape the stories we make up individually and collectively about the past and the future. This misunderstanding is in fact an egregious misrepresentation of Freud's and especially Jung's radical discovery of unconscious dynamics, which is evident in his situating their work within a humanistic perspective. See for example Chapter 7, "The Humanist Revolution," and especially p. 275 and pp. 278–279.

To his question, then, *The Frankenstein Prophecies* presents Victor Frankenstein not only as an emblem of a most dangerous god, but also as a god who not only does not know what he wants, but also does not know who he is, a flawed god who is blind to his own darkness.

While my criticism of Harari's perspective is a defense of unconscious dynamics, I am not dismissing the valid critiques that have been made of this idea. See, for example, Paul Ricoeur's book, *Freud and Philosophy: An Essay on Interpretation* (1970) as well as Susan Rowland's excellent book *Jung as a Writer* (2005). In addition, see my book *The Wounded Researcher: Research with Soul in Mind* (2007) for an extended critical discussion of the theme of unconscious dynamics.

Regarding how Jung understands unconscious dynamics see, for example *Memories, Dreams, Reflections*. Speaking of our obligations to attend to the images of the unconscious, he says, "Insight into them must be converted into an ethical obligation" (1965, p. 193). In this context, Question Seven of *The Frankenstein Prophecies*, which focuses on a Mary Shelley's work as a prophecy of a new and radical ethics in the Monster's tale is based within a Jungian psychological perspective. See also Jung's seminal essay, "On the Nature of the Psyche," which has had a profound influence on my work. In that long essay, he says regarding unconscious dynamics that they question the validity of our conscious knowledge "in an altogether different and more menacing way than it had ever been by the critical procedures of epistemology" (Jung, 1960, CW 8: para. 358). In that passage Jung also acknowledges that the presence and impact of unconscious dynamics not only has not been accepted, there has also been an outcry against it from all sides. Harari is a prime example of this dismissal albeit in a very subtle form. Unconscious dynamics shape his sober warnings about the dangers of technology by framing his account within the scientific perspective, which he regards, however, as a means of our salvation.

Question Four

OUT OF AFRICA TO THE MOON

Is Mary Shelley's story a prophecy of creating a new species of humankind?

Zombies and astronauts

George Romero's first Zombie film *Night of the Living Dead* premiered in 1968, a year before the first moon landing. Ten years later, his second Zombie film pitted Zombies against consumers who have sought refuge in a shopping mall. Both films portray the terrifying horror of the Zombies, but the second film has an ironic quality to it as it displays a similarity between Zombies and the consumer character of contemporary culture discussed in the previous question. In this question I explore the connection among astronauts and Zombies. Victor Frankenstein's dream was to use the powers of science and the technology of his time to create a new race of beings that would not be condemned to death. It was a noble dream in service to human kind. His creation, however, was not what he imagined, and the Monster he made has lived on in multiple guises to haunt our collective imagination. Zombies are an image of Victor Frankenstein's dream as nightmare. They are an unexpected offspring, the dark twin of his Monster.

Is the astronaut a figure who preserves the purity of Victor Frankenstein's dream and work by taking flight from its monstrous, unintended and undesired consequences, as Victor himself fled from his Monster?

Indeed, while astronauts are not immune to death in their leap into space, they are the first exemplar of a new species of humanity that not only preserves Frankenstein's dream but also continues and amplifies it.

Liftoff

On July 16, 1969, at Kennedy Space Center, Florida, three American Astronauts ride a Saturn V Rocket into space bound for the Moon. They are not the first of their kind to break the umbilical cord of gravity that ties us to the Earth, nor are they the first of their kind to go as far as the Moon. But four days later on July 20, 1969 Neil Armstrong, one of the three astronauts, is the first of our kind to step onto the lunar surface and impress a footprint into its dust. On that date he takes "one small step for man" and with him we take "one giant leap for mankind."

Is that footprint a turning point in human history?

Neil Armstrong, Buzz Aldrin, Michael Collins have names and histories. They have families and belong to communities. They are like us and we share the triumph of their achievement.

But it took eight days to get to the moon and return to Earth and in that time Armstrong, Aldrin and Collins did what no other human being has ever done. On the way to the moon and on the return they lived a weightless existence, and on the lunar surface whose gravity lessened their body weight they lived a much lighter existence. Weightless, they floated in their space capsules and lighter on the moon the steps taken by Armstrong and Aldrin were great bounding leaps across the lunar world.

In their epic journey to another world they were free of the pull of gravity. They were unencumbered by the weight of their bodies. They shed for a while the husk of flesh.

Living a disembodied life they seemed almost but not quite like Angels!

Who did land on the Moon?

Whose footprint marks its surface?

Was that event a moment when a new species of human being was being born?

In 1609 Galileo traveled to the moon as a disembodied telescopic eye. In 1969, Neil Armstrong stood on its surface. That step is the pivotal moment when *Homo sapiens* becomes *Homo astronauticus.* [1]

Twelve astronauts eventually landed on the lunar surface. These dozen men are the forerunners of a very small tribe, harbingers of a new kind of human being. But to make that journey and to be in the alien, airless world of the Moon, the human body of *Homo sapiens* had to be redesigned. All human actions had to be translated into their anatomical structures and physiological functions. The specimen body was the blueprint for that design.

Watching that momentous achievement on July 20, 1969, Earth begins to slip away as the natural habitat of the specimen body finds its home on the moon. Victor Frankenstein's dream and work become cosmic in that moment. Neil Armstrong's words were prescient. The giant leap of mankind was a leap into becoming a new species of *Homo sapiens.*

Homo astronauticus is a lunar species!

Was it also a first step into lunacy?

The first moon landing was and remains not only a splendid achievement but also an inspiration that still can take one's breath away. The irony however is that the felt sense that one's breath has been taken away by some awesome event is a human experience that makes sense on the Earth and not on the moon. Here on Earth breathing as a human activity is a matter of pausing between the moments of inspiration and expiration. On the moon this human activity had already been translated into the technical function of respiration. Indeed, all human activities had to be translated in this way. Imagine if Neil Armstrong after his first step on a new world looked around and, disappointed at the dull almost colorless barren surface, said his heart was broken.

"Hello Houston we have a problem."

A broken heart is a real human experience, for which an EKG machine is not the measure. A human heart can be broken in love, or it can slowly splinter into fragments in long periods of loneliness. But in sorrow or loneliness one does not need or even wish to consult a cardiologist. One might in fact turn to the poets or someone whose work has explored the depths of the human condition.

A heart attack, on the other hand, is no time for a poet, and in that instance a cardiologist who knows the specimen body is needed.

The body of *Homo astronauticus* is the specimen body created for that unique band of brothers who have stepped onto a new world. The moon, as the appropriate place for the specimen body to be, is the place where the special conditions for its appearance on the Earth, as in illness, have become the norm. On that new world we have taken one small step away from who we have been as *Homo sapiens* and one giant leap toward what we are becoming, *Homo astronauticus*. In that leap are we becoming lunatics?

Between Earth and the Moon

There is a moment in the journey to the moon when the astronaut is as far away from Earth as he or she is from the Moon. It is a moment when one can decide to turn back or to go on. We have made that choice and in that continuation of this leap into space we are uncoupling Victor Frankenstein's dream from the Earth, freeing it from its gravity, its gravitas, lifting it into the clouds.

Homo astronauticus is a leap in evolution engineered by a Promethean mind. The astronaut is the first step toward a new sense of what it means to be human, a step whose ultimate goal is to be fully free of the weight of embodiment and its stench of corruption, decay and the specter of death. That goal is the dream of Victor Frankenstein's who, in Mary Shelley's story, is proclaimed as the modern Prometheus. On that first lunar journey halfway toward a moon landing *Homo astronauticus* was continuing a journey that began when our species *Homo sapiens* evolved approximately 200,000 years ago in East Africa. For two hundred millennia up to approximately 10,000 years ago there were still several different variations of the genus *Homo* of which our species *Homos sapiens* was one. Today we are the only species of the genus *Homo*. [2]

As before so now, there are already several different species alongside *Homo astronauticus* and we will explore them shortly. Before we leave the lunar world, however, we should listen again to those words Neil Armstrong spoke as he took that first step not out of Africa but beyond Earth, and to the connection between those words and the symbol of the moon.

"One small step for man, one giant leap for mankind!"

These are the first words from a new world spoken by *Homo astronauticus*. On the launch pad in 1969 *Homo astronauticus* departs Earth as a masculine being who leaves the feminine behind.[3]

The specimen body engineered for the moon world is basically genderless. For example, in terms of its technical functioning as a pump, the heart of a man and a woman is anatomically the same.[4] Neil Armstrong's words seep with irony. The one small step for man and that one giant leap for mankind are spoken on behalf of mankind by a man whose specimen body is genderless. It is a journey in which the choice of Victor Frankenstein to exclude woman from the act of creation is proclaimed as being realized on the moon.[5]

Dreaming in space

The words of *Homo astronauticus* spoken in a new world extend Victor Frankenstein's dream to the moon and beyond. A dream of the Promethean spectator mind unbound from Earth, it repeats Victor Frankenstein's god like work of creating life apart from the feminine. The Monster was the product of that unnatural act. Is *Homo astronauticus* a descendant of Victor's Monster, a new form of life engineered by the powers of science and technology which might, as Victor Frankenstein himself feared regarding his Monster, endanger all of humanity?

When Frankenstein reneges on his promise to his Monster to make him a mate, ripping her to pieces and throwing the remnants of her body into the deep, dark, cold waters of a Scottish lake, he does so by the light of the moon. That light, which awakened him to the horrors of his dream, drove him mad. Lunar light had no place in Victor's dream, the dream of a solar mind.

On July 20, 1969, the first step taken by Neil Armstrong left its footprint on the moon. It is a human footprint but it is not our footprint. It was made by another species of us. It is the footprint of *Homo astronauticus* stamped into the dust of the lunar world as Armstrong, the first of his kind but not the last, made his leap for all mankind. The Monster's mate who was torn to pieces by his maker in the light of the moon was stamped into the lunar surface under that first step. Beneath the space boot of the astronaut, Victor Frankenstein's madness has become normalized. That footprint is the Monster's mate's grave marker. "One small step for man, one giant leap for mankind" is her dirge.

But is it her dirge unsung in an airless alien world?

Films often pick up on the unimagined and even unimaginable depths of the collective mind. They pick up what is unsung, unsaid, unheard. The films in the *Alien* series are an example. In these films the feminine, which has been buried in the deep, cold waters of the Promethean mind and consigned to dust in the lunar world, returns.

The image of the feminine in these films is quite unlike the dismissed feminine in Victor Frankenstein's work. Neither charmingly naïve and docile, as he describes Elizabeth Lavenza, nor an unintended sacrifice to his dreams and his work, nor even the horrific image of the corpse of his dead mother in one of his dreams, the feminine does not simply die. The feminine does not simply sink into oblivion.

In the *Alien* films the feminine that had no place in Victor Frankenstein's creation of life and has also been exiled in the new lunar world of *Homo astronauticus* returns with a vengeance. In her alien presence, she is the Monster's mate who has risen up from those cold, deep waters of the Promethean mind. She is huge, powerful, destructive and terrifying in her monstrous appearance. She is Victor Frankenstein's worst nightmare who, as the film suggests, is waiting in the far reaches beyond Earth for *Homo astronauticus*. [6]

Frankenstein as Prophecy

Homo astronauticus is the first in a line of development that not only continues Victor Frankenstein's god like dream to create life, but also extends it to creating a new species of *Homo sapiens*. The tools of science and technology that we now possess especially in genetic and computer technologies are increasing at such an exponential rate that we are already leaping beyond the boundaries of natural evolution. Through genetic manipulation cloning can now make copies of organs of the human body and we can even clone entire individual organisms. These powers are also routinely employed to create new species of plants, animals and viruses.

While the intentions behind this work are as admirable as those of Victor Frankenstein, the dangers are palpable. Who, for example, makes the choices about the use of these powers is a political issue. In addition, moral and ethical questions suffuse our good intentions. Because we have the power to do such things, should we do them?[7]

As we continue this story in Question Five, the creation of another new species of us is moving toward the dream of one day creating a new species of life that has finally taken leave of the body. On a path from astronauts to angels in clouds, the question of whether we should continue to exercise our god like powers is being reframed in a chilling way. In continuing the god like dream of Victor Frankenstein are we harbingers of the last generations of humankind? This question is one that makes the prophetic character of Mary Shelley's story truly terrifying.

Notes

1 See my *Technology as Symptom and Dream* (1989/2006) for an extended discussion of this event.

2 See Question Three, note 14 regarding Harari (2011) *Sapiens: A Brief History of Humankind.*

3 Regarding this split between the masculine and the feminine see my discussion of the astronaut and the anorexic in *Technology as Symptom and Dream*, Chapter four and especially pp. 170–173. In that chapter I describe the history of the abandoned body and its shadows—See Fig. 5.1, p. 134. This earlier book anticipates in many ways the themes of *The Frankenstein Prophecies*, especially regarding the body. It tells the same story of the discovery and creation of the specimen body, the anatomical body, but tells it through the lens of Mary Shelley's riveting and pivotal story. *The Frankenstein Prophecies* returns to and re-members the history presented in *Technology as Symptom and Dream* in a dramatic way.

Moreover, insofar as every book when it is finished is still not done and what is left over waits for its moment, the connection between the astronaut and the anorexic implied in Neil Armstrong's words was already latent in Galileo's telescopic exploration of the moon in 1609. Describing the dream of technology, I wrote the following: "In dreaming this dream we have in effect declared that matter no longer matters. Small wonder, then, that in the midst of plenty, the anorexic starves. Indeed the more we try to force-feed her, to put flesh back on her bones, the closer she comes to death. It is as if through her battle with food we are given a symbol that the material world we have created is a dead matter, a world which cannot sustain us" (1989/2006, pp. 170–171).

In 1609 Galileo's telescopic eye leaves the body behind. In 1969 the first astronaut whose body has been re-designed for the lunar world steps onto the moon. In 1689 the first medical diagnosis of anorexia appears when the English physician Richard Morton describes a female patient as a "skeleton clad only in skin." In 1969 that starving skeleton is left behind on an increasingly imperiled earth.

For a good clinical overview of anorexia, see the classic work by Hilda Bruch (1979), *The Golden Cage: The Enigma of Anorexia Nervosa*.

4 Indeed, this was the point that William Harvey made in his 1628 text where the heart is first described as a pump and as the same for all creatures. That he dedicated his revolutionary anatomical text to King Charles I of England is truly a piece of historical irony because as Charles was about to be beheaded by the forces of Oliver Cromwell he said, "A subject and a sovereign are clear different things" (Romanyshyn, 2001, p. 139). For a full discussion of this quote see pp. 138–141.

5 On the Apollo 12 mission in November 1969, Pete Conrad demonstrated that on the lunar world Galileo's law of falling bodies, according to which all bodies fall equally fast, is true. Just as the specimen body finds its home on the moon, so too does this law of physics. Both examples indicate that we have adopted an astrophysical point of view regarding our bodies and nature. The monstrous side of this view was displayed in Hiroshima. President Truman said as much when he said we have brought the power of the sun to Earth. Here is the Promethean mind in all its modern radiant darkness.

6 There is a scene in *Aliens*, the 1986 sequel to *Alien* (1979), when the character Ellen Ripley played by Sigourney Weaver, encounters the Queen of the alien monsters. In this encounter the Alien Queen wants to protect the eggs of her unborn offspring from Ripley's weapons. Although they eventually do battle, there is moment when Ripley seems to understand the desire of the Alien Queen, a moment that suggests a tenuous bond of compassion between Ripley and the monstrous form of the Alien Queen. But that moment is short lived and the Alien Queen is destroyed.

The similarity between the *Alien* films and Mary Shelley's story rests on the same moral dilemma. In terms of their difference from us, a monster, judged as Other, and condemned to death opens a cycle of ongoing violence. The film, however, might also extend Mary Shelley's story. Victor's Monster promised that he and his mate would not procreate. It was a promise that was a sacrifice of the future. In the film, the monster's protection of her unborn children suggests that the feminine excluded from the act of creation offers a path of redemption when and if the sense of a future is not sacrificed. Victor's Monster, born from the Promethean mind of his creator was already in his form and figure the shape of a life that has no future. The monstrous form of the Alien feminine in these films makes that theme explicit.

7 For several recent books on this issue see the following: Luke Dormehi (2017), *Thinking Machines: The Quest for Artificial Intelligence and Where It's Taking Us Next*; Richard Yonck (2017), *Heart of the Machine: Our Future in a World of Artificial Intelligence*; Bonnie Rochman (2017), *How Genetic Technologies Are Changing the Way We Have Kids*; Adam Piore (2017), *The Body Builders: Inside the Science of the Engineered Human*; Mark O'Connell (2017), *To be a Machine: Adventures Among Cyborgs, Utopians, Hackers, and the Futurists Solving the Modest problem of Death*.

Question Five

FROM ASTRONAUTS TO ANGELS IN CLOUDS

Is Mary Shelley's story a prophecy of the last generations of humankind?

The thread of technology

Ray Kurzweil's thought is a prophetic and logical extension of Victor Frankenstein's Promethean dream because in his writings Frankenstein's dream ultimately leads to more than just creating new life. Kurzweil's work suggests that the thread of our technology is toward the creation of a new species whose life is disembodied and in the clouds. For him there is no question that the body will be jettisoned at a point he calls the Singularity, when human kind will transcend biology. Moreover, he connects this "angelic" state with taking leave of the earth. The astronaut, which, as we saw in Question Four, is modeled on the specimen body that was the blueprint for Victor Frankenstein's creation of the Monster, is the first step that leads to angels in clouds. It is this specimen body, then, that threads the way from Victor Frankenstein's dream to Ray Kurzweil's fantastical predictions.

But as one reads his work, one has to wonder if Kurzweil realizes that the monstrous body that Victor Frankenstein made is the biological specimen body that would be jettisoned in the moment of Singularity. One has to ask if he acknowledges or at least recognizes that his dream was born in Victor Frankenstein's laboratory. If he does not, then the dangers of Victor Frankenstein's Promethean dream remain hidden.

The Frankenstein Prophecies addresses these dangers. In this question we describe two other variations of our species *Homo sapiens*, which are the prophetic progeny of Victor Frankenstein's Monster, and which currently coexist with *Homo astronauticus*.

Frankenstein as Prophecy

WWW

At the computer terminal Victor Frankenstein's question—Why does anyone have to die?—is not only being answered, it is also being radically reframed. His flight from death is becoming a flight from the flesh itself. At the computer terminal a new species of *Homo sapiens* freed from the weight of embodiment is being created. The computer terminal is another step toward the cloud where no one will ever die. In the cloud no one will die because *Homo sapiens* will have disappeared.

The spectator mind at the computer screen is a disembodied self whose identity is terminal. Its terminal identity is not, however, a diagnosis of a fatal condition.[1] On the contrary it is a description of a new species of *Homo sapiens* that we might call, with a bit of a wink, *Homo digitalis*.

Homo digitalis seems an apt description since digital, derived from a Latin root meaning finger, is a term that has become ubiquitous when describing the environment of the world-wide-web. The digital world is a world that we tap into with our fingers, which is quite a different way of handling the world, of taking hold of what is at hand in our daily embodied engagement with the things of the world that surround us.

The term digitalis itself is the name for a group of plants including the foxgloves whose corollas look like fingers. The seeds and dried leaves of foxglove plants are used as a heart stimulant to regulate and control the irregular and often too fast pumping action of the heart in cases of atrial fibrillation. As a new species of us, *Homo digitalis* is at home in the web, just as *Homo astronauticus* is at home on the moon. His or her heartbeat is regulated to keep pace and be in synch with the fast paced rhythms of the digital world where one can be on line 24/7 pecking away with fox-gloved fingers.[2]

Homo digitalis is an evolutionary step beyond *Homo astronauticus*. But just as Neanderthals and *Homo sapiens* once co-existed, the astronaut in his space capsule and the computer person in the world-wide-web co-exist as two new species of humanity.

Homo digitalis is a hybrid species with its own unique features and features of the specimen body retained from *Homo astronauticus*. If one were to imagine a future scenario in which the archaic remains of a *Homo digitalis* were discovered, one might find him or her at a computer terminal with the fox-gloved hands of *Homo digitalis* and the pumping heart of *Homo astronautics* that had stopped working. On the screen, one might even find a final message, perhaps appended to the title page of Mary Shelley's story, wondering if his kind has suffered the same fate as Victor's Monster.

Typing at the computer screen, one is—as I am myself at this moment—already a member of the species *Homo digitalis*. Finger pecking at the keys—or, if one is adept enough to type with many fox-gloved digits—a gap emerges between this action and the slow hand holding the pen that lingers over the page.

The page and the screen! The hand that writes the words and the fingers that peck the keys!

The blank screen and the blank page are not the same, and it is undeniable that the computer fingers of *Homo digitalis* are quicker and more efficient than the writing hand of *Homo sapiens*.

The blank page, especially in its stark whiteness can, like Melville's white whale, inspire terror. The writer paused with pen in hand has to wait to see what might rise up from the depths when he or she penetrates the page with a mark. What might surface as one lances the page with the pen? The writing hand that hovers over the blank page cultivates patience and endurance. The blank page slows one's thinking down.

The pecking fingers before the blank screen are quicker. Such fingers are convenient and useful for the wide expanses of the digital ocean that swells with wave upon wave of information. One has to be quick and to some degree indifferent to the content so that one can jab at a number of the offerings, sampling as it were this and that from the plethora of enticing possibilities. The pecking fingers of *Homo digitalis* are at home in front of a blank screen. Unlike the one facing a blank page who is like a whale hunter waiting to capture some treasure from the dark depths below the surface, *Homo digitalis* has been created to surf the digital ocean of information that spreads itself in a world wide web that covers the globe.

But so what?

Does the difference matter?

Does not the blank screen offer advantages that are undeniable?

These questions are not meant to challenge the benefits of our technological creations. Rather, these questions are asked so that we might pause to consider the consequences of the differences that do emerge. If we are to know where we are going, we have to understand where we are. Indeed, at critical points, there are even questions that do more than slow us down. The prophetic amplifications of Mary Shelley's story can stop us in our tracks and doing so the present moment can become a pivotal moment, a moment when something as familiar as www might become unfamiliar, seem suddenly strange and perhaps even uncanny.

Fascinated by all the possibilities of our technological wonders, are we failing to think about the consequences and thus repeating Victor Frankenstein's story?[3]

The computer screen is more than our window on the world.[4] *Homo digitalis* looks out at more than any local scene that a window displays. At the computer terminal the whole world has been opened up as a spectacle that can be seen and observed from afar. Indeed, in our technological version of paradise, Steve Job's Apple has so magnified the spectacle that it has become boundless. The space and time of the world have lost their local character.

Where is the sky in the digital world? Where is the earth? Where is the depth of this space? Its vertically has been usurped by the horizontality of an almost infinite expanse that eclipses or nearly so the local scale of time and space where the sky above marks the daily and seasonal rounds of life, and where the earth below bears witness to our presence in the roads paved, the gardens made, the crop fields planted and the grave stones that memorialize the dead.

There is no weather in the digital world, no seasons and no grave markers. *Homo digitalis* needs no clothing; no one catches a chill or a cold in the digital world. No one ever dies there. And no one can pray because in the eclipse of the vertical in the almost limitless expanse of the digital world the gods have been ex-plained away.[5] Or, more to the point, as Mary Shelley's story prophesizes, they have been replaced by us.

If there are no gods that set the boundary of human life is anything possible?

If there are no gods are there any limits to our Promethean spectator mind unchained at the computer terminal where even the sky is no longer the limit?

Boundless and unchained where is the community of others when we meet at and through the terminal, where all of us now have a terminal identity, an image presence on a screen that has no haptic sense, a space where, while we are in touch, we are quite specifically out of touch with each other?[6] At the computer screen one is an image, which, not weighted with flesh, floats free and can be anywhere in the digital world.[7]

At the computer screen one is a spectacle of a disembodied self. We can see each other and hear and talk with and to each other but we cannot touch each other or be touched. In addition, there is no whiff of the other's presence, no scent of the other, which taps into our mammalian roots and which is a radical bond of intimacy between people. And, perhaps most importantly, although each of us can befriend a magnitude of others, no one of any of us can kiss the other in the digital world.

But how many Facebook friends does one need?

How many friends can one honestly have?

Or, perhaps we should ask what friendship means to a member of the species *Homo digitalis*?[8]

In digital space does *Homo digitalis* ever regret that some one-eyed son of a bitch has invented an instrument to be alone together?[9]

Is there time to consider these issues?

At the computer terminal we surf the wide expanse of the digital ocean at almost the speed of light.

Can we make time for these issues in a world in which we are virtually on line 24/7?

Conditioned by the bleeps and buzzes of our digital devices, is there time for silence when the pace of disembodied images on the screen feels like an injunction to keep the flow of words moving?

Images without flesh have no anchor in the body. On the computer screen the field of fleshy engagement between self and other in the non-digital world is absent. The arch of an eyebrow, the tilt of one's head, the hands rubbed together while speaking to or being spoken to by the other, are silent companions of the word, the fleshy gestural field that dresses language. In the digital world the fleshy garment of language is shrinking.

On the street, in the pub, at the political rally words are more than matters of mind. They make sense because they are sensed. In the non-digital world, language is a drama that is spoken and enacted. In the non-digital world we impregnate each other with meaning and desire. Language as an embodied gestural field is a web of fleshy entanglements with all its ambiguities and mess, with all its spoken and unspoken gestured appeals, where the folly and absurdity of trying to say what one means and to mean what one says is nakedly displayed through the body, where the lies of a hidden mind betray themselves on a blushing face.

What is truth in the digital world, when even the images on the screen can be photo shopped?

Can a person tell a lie in the digital world where words are unhinged from the flesh?

Would one be able to tell if a person is telling a lie or speaking the truth?

Words of mind unhinged from flesh are tricky, but the body does not lie if you are practiced in reading its gestures. Descartes's famous dictum, "I think, therefore, I am," might be the first lie suited to the digital world, where the thinking mind is virtually invisible.

The constant chatter on our digital devices keeps silence at bay. But silence is the portal through which the unspoken in the spoken enters. Psychotherapists who attend to the body and good poker players linger at this portal. They attend to the "tells." They pick up on these subtle social clues.

People with autism and Asperger syndrome are not able to read such clues. Their plight is dramatically portrayed *The Accountant* (2016). A key point of the film shows that insofar as the medical establishment and culture in general diagnose such people, we see their difference from us only in negative terms. In short, we marginalize them. They become "monstrous."[10]

Are these pathologies the tell of the Monster on the margins, the shadow side of *Homo digitalis* at the computer terminal?[11]

The first signs of autism and Asperger syndrome appear in very young children.

Are these children the marginal offspring of the Monster made and feared by his maker Victor Frankenstein?

Are they prophecies of what we are becoming as a new species born with terminal identity?

At the computer terminal where we take leave of our senses does the body that is left behind become a diagnosable commodity?

In the digital world we are radically transforming our relationship to nature, time, community, language and the body. Doing so, we are not only continuing Victor Frankenstein's god like dream to create life, we are amplifying that dream at a rapid and dizzying pace.

As Victor Frankenstein does his work his primary value is how quickly it can be done. Speed is essential. In this regard, as a new kind of god he is quite like Hermes, the winged and quick footed one who bridges the gap between humans and the gods to carry the messages of the gods to humanity. But there is no bridge anymore. There is no need for one because Victor Frankenstein has replaced the gods. *Homo digitalis* is a personification of Victor Frankenstein's dream. It is an unrecognized and unacknowledged image of what we are becoming.

We are as gods in this digital space!

Creators of ourselves, makers of a new kind of being that makes a spectacle of itself, a being who, having sundered the erotic bonds of the sensual flesh and the sensuous world with all its appeals and seductions, its temptations to linger and to find in the moment the splendor of the simple, the miracle in the mundane, and who, now floating free outside the envelope of time, and having forgotten that every present moment is cradled within a past that lingers, haunts and casts its presence in the present, and a future that bewitches and beguiles the present moment and companions it forward, we are becoming timeless and perhaps even dream of becoming eternal.

But as we peck away in digital space, does the monster wait in exile haunting us with his marginal presence?

Angels in the digital cloud

Ray Kurzweil, perhaps the most daring futurist, who now directs Google's Artificial Intelligence program, is dreaming Victor Frankenstein's dream forward. His writings seed the dreams of the collective mind with an image of another new species. Kurzweil maps out the path toward that goal in *The Singularity Is Near: When Humans Transcend Biology* (2005).[12] That he calls the moment when humans will transcend biology a singularity is significant because the term, which is borrowed from physics, describes the moment when we encounter the boundaries of our knowledge.

Until recently, physicists believed that it was not possible to know what is beyond that boundary. But drawing upon the work of Stephen Hawking, Kurzweil makes a daring leap into the unknown to probe the present state of our computer and genetic knowledge and, without much of a pause, dream it forward.[13] So, for example, graphing how the rate of technological acceleration is exponential and not linear, he claims that by 2045 our technological powers will become self-evolving to be beyond our control. At this point the future of *Homo sapiens* becomes rather chilling as Kurzweil imagines a new age, which heralds the coming of a new species of humanity.

A primary theme in Kurzweil's work is that the process of natural evolution is much too slow to keep pace with the exponential growth of our computer and genetic knowledge. This exponential growth means that our knowledge is doubling every ten years. To give a simple example of this exponential scale, if you were to save a penny each day for a hundred days you will end with a dollar. But if you could double each penny every following day so that one becomes two and two becomes four and four becomes eight and so on, in thirty days you would have $5,368,709.12.

If Kurzweil is right about the exponential pace of technological knowledge, and there is some evidence to support that view, then are we becoming the creators of our own demise as *Homo sapiens*?

Frankenstein's Monster was the agent of his maker's destruction.

Is the marriage of our computer and genetic technologies the Monster we are creating without careful regard for the consequences?

Kurzweil, however, seems unaware of this prophetic link between his dream and the dream that inspired Victor Frankenstein. Fascinated by this exponential growth in our technological knowledge, perhaps he is just indifferent to the connection. Whichever is the case, he so fully embraces the possibilities of these technologies that he says the destiny of the entire universe is ultimately to be saturated with our intelligence.

There is more than a whiff of hubris in this view. At the Singularity it is not just we who will be radically transformed: all of creation will be changed. Kurzweil writes: "Once we saturate the matter and energy in the universe with intelligence, it will 'wake up,' be conscious, and sublimely intelligent" (Kurzweil, 2005, p. 375).

> This is the ultimate destiny of the Singularity and of the universe … . Our civilization will … expand outward, turning all the dumb matter and energy we encounter into sublimely intelligent—transcendent—matter and energy. So in a sense, we can say that the Singularity will ultimately infuse the universe with spirit.
>
> *(Kurzweil, 2005, pp. 21, 389)*

There is a tantalizing bit of irony in Kurzweil's words. In 1900 Freud described dreams as wish fulfillments of repressed desires. In this way dreams were guardians of sleep. Victor Frankenstein's first dream after his Monster has awakened and he has fled from the horror he has created is a nightmare. The implication is that his wish to become a new creator god was even too much for him to stay asleep to its dangers. His dream seems to have had a deeper wisdom than the intentions of his Promethean mind.[14]

Kurzweil, however, is so fully ensorcelled by his dream to saturate the universe with our intelligence that he seems oblivious to or at least unconcerned about any possible nightmarish consequences of waking up the universe. Indeed, he enthusiastically wants to wake up the dumb, sleepy matter of the universe. His sunny, unquestioned optimism is underscored by the fact that the last words in his book say that as we increasingly transcend the limits of our biology, progress toward this moment "will continue until the entire universe is at our fingertips" (Kurzweil, 2005, p. 487).

But whose fingertips?

Are they the fox-gloved fingertips of *Homo digitalis*?

According to Ray Kurzweil the hardware and software needed to fully emulate human intelligence is progressing so rapidly that by the end of the 2020s we can expect computers to pass the Turing Test, indicating intelligence indistinguishable from that of biological humans. When that happens, the "you" that you are will no longer be able to tell the difference between yourself and a computer.[15] If by the 2020s we have quite adapted to our terminal identity at the computer screen, then *Homo digitalis* is the most likely candidate to fulfill Kurzweil's dream of that moment when we will be able to tap into the universe. Given that Kurzweil's dream leads to the transcendence of our biology, to the eclipse of our being human beings who are embodied, then what is the fate of *Homo digitalis?* Are we as *Homo digitalis* to be replaced by another species?

From terminal identity to the Singularity

When the pace of computer and genetic technologies is so rapid that each new development increasingly enthralls us, will it still matter that we are unable to tell the difference between human and machine intelligence?

And, with the promise on the horizon of ascending into the digital cloud, will the fate of *Homo digitalis* still matter?

These questions take us deeper into Kurzweil's dream. The arc of his work indicates that as our genetic and computer technologies continue to transform us, he says there will be a point where we will be human even if we are not biological.

Human even if we are not biological!

This is an incredible statement and an extremely daring and some might say even outrageous claim. It calls for our attention.

Elaborting his statement, Kurzweil says:

> This will be the next step in evolution, the next high-level paradigm shift ... Most of the intelligence of our civilization will ultimately be non-biological. By the end of this century, it will be trillions of trillions of times more powerful than human intelligence.[16]
>
> *(2005, p. 30)*

Between the 2020s and the end of the century the quality of being embodied will increasingly no longer be a part of being human. On the contrary, the quality that will mark one as human will be intelligence. Biological, instinctual, embodied intelligence, which evolved in relation to nature, will be replaced by digital intelligence apart from nature.

Nearly four hundred years ago Descartes imagined this possibility. "I think, therefore, I am," was his philosophical expression of this vision. A pithy summary of the spectator mind in flight from the flesh, it anticipates Kurzweil's bold claim. But his claim goes far beyond Descartes in three significant ways.

First, the philosophical idea has become a scientific fact, or at least the claim to be so with the exponential advances in the areas of genetics and computers.

Second, Kurzweil's claim extends well beyond the mind of an "I" who thinks to the "We" of a collective world-wide-web computer mind and its trove of all human intelligence.

And third, Kurzweil's claim is a radical shift from thinking as an activity of a philosophical mind to thinking as a matter of the bits and bytes of data of a computational mind. It is a change from thinking as a meditative act to thinking as a calculative act.[17]

And yet, what still links Kurzweil's bold claim to the philosophical vision of Descartes is that they both split matter and mind. Both imagine a division between a material, visible biological body with its limited instinctual kind of intelligence, and a disembodied, invisible mind with its speculative kind of intelligence. In spite of this link, however, Kurzweil's claim boldly goes where no one has quite gone before.

The mind as an invisible ghost in the machine body has been one of the most vivid images of the split between mind and matter made so long ago by Descartes. With Kurzweil the ghost is no longer invisible. It is the digital web mind housed in the computer that sits on our desks and is serviced by us as *Homo digitalis*, or the tablet that we, as *Homo digitalis*, carry with us. Computers and i-pads are the bones, as it were, of the heretofore invisible mind, the exoskeleton of the hardware and software of the mind-machine, which in a piece of evolutionary irony reverses the natural processes of evolution that transformed the external shells into internal frames. So, to return to the question above regarding that moment when the universe will be at our fingertips, who or what is it whose fingertips are being imagined?

As I suggested above, it appears to be the fingertips of *Homo digitalis* furiously tapping the keys with fox-gloved hands that will ultimately infuse the universe with spirit.

In this scenario the bold, even inflated quality of Kurzweil's work begins to stand out.

Who is master and who is slave?

Acknowledging an often expressed concern about his claim, or shall we say dream, Kurzweil says it "does not imply the end of biological intelligence." While that sounds a bit reassuring, what follows reaffirms his claim. Biological intelligence, by which he means the instinctual intelligence of the body as matter separate from mind, will not end, but it will be "thrown from its perch of evolutionary superiority." Moreover, while "Our civilization will remain human," this fall of biological intelligence from its high perch will create a civilization that "in many ways will be more exemplary of what we regard as human than it is today." But lest we become too quickly enthralled by this prospect we have to attend once more to his insistence that "our understanding of the term (human) will move beyond its biological origins" (Kurzweil, 2005, p. 30).

There is no mistaking Kurzweil's intention. For him what is exemplary about being human is our ever increasing engineered capacity for intelligence. In this context, being human ultimately has little if anything at all to do with being embodied. In fact, the body is a drag on the goal of reaching our full potential as human beings. The body ages and eventually dies. Victor Frankenstein was horrified by these facts. Ray Kurzweil is not horrified by them. On the contrary, he is confident and convinced that that horror can and will and even must be overcome. In his confidence he is taking Victor Frankenstein's dream and dreaming it forward.

Kurzweil's confidence in his bold claim is persuasive.

Who would not want to defeat the Grim Reaper, or at least postpone death for as long as possible?

Who would not want to erase the marks of ageing and decay and preserve the vigor and beauty of youth?

Now that we have the technological powers to do so, it is so tempting, as you read Kurzweil, to believe that the god like powers we seem to possess to shape and direct the natural processes of evolution make their use not only inevitable but also obligatory. Indeed, the morally imperative tone in his work, which echoes that of Victor Frankenstein, is where the fictive figure of Frankenstein crosses the threshold into fact.

But what lingers in the background of this creation of an exemplary human?

And what might be the relation between such an exemplary human that Kurzweil claims we are becoming, and the embodied human being with its biological intelligence that we still are, even at the computer terminal?

Will the biological intelligence of the embodied human being become so inferior to the enhanced intelligence of the exemplary human being that a version of the slave–master relationship will emerge?

Might we with all our biological limitations, from the slow pace at which we process information to becoming weary and in need of periodic rests, awake one day to find ourselves enslaved to our computer stations in service to the task of infusing the universe with the world-wide-web intelligence of our masters, the enhanced, exemplary humans?

While this scenario is a possibility that lies on the margins of Ray Kurzweil's dream, it is a possibility already anticipated. As the species *Homo digitalis* are we not already slaves to our computers, addicted to the glut of information that pervades the web, pecking away at the keys trying to feed a seemingly endless hunger not only for more and more information, but also to assuage the loneliness of our terminal identities?

Kurzweil's work builds on that possibility. His claim, his vision, is his creation dream, and he is as committed to it as his ancestor Victor Frankenstein was committed to his creation dream.

And yet even at the computer terminal it is still possible to click the off button. *Homo digitalis* is still more than a gadget.[18]

But for how long?

Spiritual machines

For Kurzweil version 2.0 of the human body "represents the continuation of a long standing trend in which we grow more intimate with our technology" (Kurzweil, 2005, p. 309). The word intimate suggests that as version 2.0 is engineered into version 3.0, which he claims will be achieved in the 2030s and 2040s, the kind of being we now are—human body version 1.0 with its biological intelligence—will feel quite at home with being a cyborg. He or she, or should we say It, might even love being a cyborg.

Homo astronauticus and *Homo digitalis* are already engineered variations of Kurzweil's version 2.0 of the human body. Indeed, we have become so familiar with these two variations that we do already feel quite at home in a body engineered for the moon and beyond, and strangely quite intimate with our alienation at the computer terminal, quite comfortable with our terminal identity.

But as we move toward version 3.0 Kurzweil seems to hesitate for a moment. While he notes that "the human body version 3.0 is likely still to look human by today's standards," he adds that our "ideas of what constitutes beauty will be expanded upon over time" (Kurzweil, 2005, p. 310).

The word *likely* introduces a bit of uncertainty, which Kurzweil directly ties to the issue of beauty. This point is instructive because for Victor Frankenstein the form, figure and especially the face of the Monster did not live up to his idea of beauty and that failure spoiled his work of creation. Kurzweil seems to recognize, as he says, that our ideas of beauty will have to expand, but in the context of the Frankenstein story that awareness takes on something closer to an injunction. With exponential genetic advances steadily increasing our capacities to experiment with multiple variations of the human form, our ideas of beauty will *have to be* expanded over time.

Beauty, as we say, is in the eye of the beholder, but that eye is always embedded within a cultural matrix. As that matrix changes, the idea of what is beautiful also shifts. What does not change, however, is that a culturally informed idea of beauty functions as an ideal that separates what is exemplary and accepted from what is excluded and marginalized even as monstrous.

The specimen body of Victor Frankenstein's Monster was itself modeled on an ideal of beauty that seems to have been in the background of his work. Albrecht Durer, the fifteenth century artist and engraver, championed the ideal of beauty to be a body that was made up of many different body parts. In one of his drawings the ideal nude figure was composed of the arms of one body, the legs of another, the chest of a third and so on. His ideal nude prefigured Victor's Monster.[19]

Durer's ideal nude and Frankenstein's Monster are bodies composed of biological parts. Kurzweil's version 3.0 is largely made up of non-biological components. But the cyborg image of version 3.0 is not a programmed robot or part of a hive mind, as portrayed, for example, in the popular Star Trek episodes about the Borg.[20] On the contrary, Kurzweil imagines his cyborgian creature as leading to a future self whose non-biological portion of intelligence will so dominate the biological portion that these future selves will be what he described in one of his works as spiritual machines.[21] As such, these future selves "will claim to have emotional and spiritual experiences, just as we do today" (Kurzweil, 2005, p. 377).

This claim has been and is the stuff of our collective dreams, and Kurzweil's work promises to transform these dreams into waking reality. Our collective dreams, which are often closer to nightmares in which cyborgs turn against humanity, are becoming our imagined future.[22] For Kurzweil, however, the darker, revolting side of this future self is quite absent, for it is a future that emerges from the technological triumph over the natural processes of evolution. In his full faith in this triumph of technology he goes on to say:

> From a practical perspective such claims will be accepted … Furthermore, these non-biological entities will be extremely intelligent, so they'll be able to convince other humans (biological, non-biological, or somewhere in between) that they are conscious. They'll have all the delicate emotional clues that convince us today that humans are conscious. They will be able to make other humans laugh and cry. And they'll get mad if others don't accept their claims.
>
> *(Kurzweil, 2005, pp. 378–379)*

This is a rather chilling prospect to imagine because laughing and crying are two quintessentially human qualities. If these spiritual machines will be able to make us laugh and cry, will they be so intelligent that they will also be able to convince us that they can laugh and cry as well? Moreover, if these future selves will get mad if we do not accept their claims, will their claims become demands? We know what the anger of Victor's Monster did when his maker refused his plea to make him a mate. Kurzweil's angry spiritual machines seem to be the nightmare version of Victor's betrayed Monster.

Singularity and beyond

At the point of Singularity whatever we have been—*Homo sapiens, Homo astronauticus, Homo digitalis*—will have evolved to the point where "we," version 3.0 of the exemplary human, will combine the traditional strengths of human intelligence with the strengths of machine intelligence and will be able to process billions of bits of information almost instantaneously and with nearly perfect accuracy without ever tiring.[23]

This future self seems to be a noble dream. But we should not forget that the values of efficiency, speed, perfection, size as a measure of the amount of information that will be processed, which calls to mind the value of size for Frankenstein in making his Monster, as well as the value of never tiring, which hints at being beyond biological death, are all values that characterized Victor Frankenstein's noble dream.

Taking note of the similarity between their dreams, a sense of caution would be prudent. This caution is not for the purpose of obstructing that dream, which in any case would be a quixotic gesture, akin to Don Quixote's tilting at windmills.[24] Rather, this caution provides a pause when, as we drift into Kurzweil's dream, we can recall how Victor Frankenstein's dream ended, which might then alter somewhat how we proceed.

Kurzweil is very specific about the direction of his dream. Beyond the point of Singularity, he foresees, "There will be no distinction post-Singularity between human and machine or between physical and virtual reality" (2005, p. 9). With these boundaries erased, "our experiences will increasingly take place in virtual environments" (2005, p. 29).

Kurzweil's post-Singularity expectations, which actually seem closer to predictions, not only point to the disappearance of the body as the differences between us and machines are eclipsed, they also point to the increasing disappearance of the natural world as its differences from virtual reality fade from memory. This erasure of the body and this dying away of the natural world are themes that linger on the margins of Mary Shelley's work as prophecies. Without that measure of caution, Kurzweil's predictions not only fulfill the prophecies in Mary Shelley's story, they carry them to their logically extreme conclusions.

At the edge of dreams

The specter of death is the shadow of embodiment and as such the body is the ultimate obstacle that stands in the way of Kurzweil's dream. To overcome that obstacle, the body has to be re-imagined, re-designed and re-created. Victor Frankenstein is the prototypical emblem of a new kind of god who, using the powers of science and technology, would fulfill that dream. Ray Kurzweil belongs to this tradition. Of the Singularity he says, "That's about as close to God as I can imagine"[25] (Kurzweil, 2005, p. 375).

Perhaps more humble than Frankenstein's dream of becoming a god, Kurzweil's dream seems more real to us because it comes pre-wrapped in the guise of scientific facts, which today are the single measure and only norm of what constitutes reality. Confident about this measure and its inevitable progress, Kurzweil never conjectures about the heritage of his spiritual machines, nor does he wonder about the name of this new species of *Homo sapiens*.

Mary Shelley's story is a re-imagining of the western story of creation in which Victor Frankenstein as the modern Prometheus replaces the Christian God of heaven. Ray Kurzweil is an updated and more powerful version of that Promethean dream. At the edge of the Singularity where he is close to being God, his spiritual machines might be the emergence of a new species of us as angels, which in the western story of creation are closer to God than us.

In Kurzweil's dream are we becoming a new kind of angel, a techno version of the Christian angel, a new species of us free of the weight of the flesh, cleansed of its pull to earth?

Homo astronauticus on the way to the moon and back approached that condition and in that encapsulated environment anticipated the angelic version of us at the edge of Kurzweil's dream. On the way to that edge all of us have been moving toward becoming advanced, enhanced versions of the astronaut floating free in space. From *Homo astronauticus* through *Homo digitalis* we are becoming *Homo angelicus*. [26]

Left behind

The intelligence of *Homo angelicus*, which seems an apt name for the ultimate image of Kurzweil's exemplary humans, is destined to dominate the embodied intelligence of those left behind.

But who are those left behind?

For Kurzweil those left behind are those who might wish to be unenhanced humans.[27]

Unenhanced humans!

The adjective does more than just qualify how Kurzweil regards those humans who might wish to remain embodied. Not quite up to Victor Frankenstein's description of his Monster as devil and demon, it does carry a negative connotation. Unenhanced points to something lacking in those left behind. It devalues who or what these unenhanced humans are compared with the enhanced beings, those who have become spiritual machines whose guise as *Homo angelicus* is now saturating the entire universe with its intelligence, with all the bits and bytes of information of the world wide webbed computer mind downloaded into the cyber cloud.

What could the unenhanced human be when measured against *Homo angelicus* as a cosmic species, as the ultimate evolved version of what we were long ago when as *Homo sapiens* we stepped out of Africa?

We are already quite use to being enhanced by the instruments of technology from eyeglasses, hearing aids to pace makers, artificial limbs and brain implants, and they do enhance the quality of our lives. Many of these familiar devices even slip more or less easily into becoming so much a part of a person that it is difficult to imagine being without them.[28]

Kurzweil's predictions build upon this familiarity. The ubiquitous cell phone is a good example. If not yet fully an intimate part of one's identity, if not yet fully identified with one's sense of self, a cell phone loops one into a globally wired world. Cell phone in hand we are a step closer to being the fully enhanced humans that Kurzweil imagines.

To test the hold of this net of devices try, for example, turning off your cell phone for a week, or even a day. As difficult as it might be to disconnect from the 24/7 cycle, it does give some indication of how much more difficult it will be to remain unenhanced in Kurzweil's world.

Weighed in the balance of *Homo angelicus* would the wish to be *un-enhanced* really carry any weight?[29]

And therein lies a danger. The binary of enhanced and unenhanced raises an ethical issue. Who makes the decision regarding one's wish to remain unenhanced and on what grounds? The ethical questions surrounding his dream to create life are quickly passed over by Victor Frankenstein and replaced by the utilitarian values of how quickly and efficiently the work can be done. The primary consequence of his rash behavior ends with the destruction of the mate he was making for his Monster to prevent any offspring, thereby in effect sterilizing him. Do such possibilities lie on the edge of Kurzweil's dream for those who wish to remain un-enhanced?

Of angels and monsters

Almost a decade before Neil Armstrong left the first footprint on the lunar world of *Homo astronauticus*, the Russian Cosmonaut Yuri Gargarin, the first man to orbit the earth in 1961, was reported to have said that he did not see any angels in outer space. Whether apocryphal or not the claim makes a key point. Before that first footprint was made the heavens were scrubbed clean of angels. They had to be if we as new gods and lords of creation are reimagining heaven to suit our image.

The angels that Gargarin did not see, those beings that disappeared with the collapse of the Christian medieval world, have returned in the retelling of that story of creation within the context of science and technology.[30] Within the context of this new story of creation, is the un-enhanced version of *Homo sapiens*, the last generation of our kind?

We are faced with a choice. Do we want a human future or a future envisioned by Kurzweil?

The Singularity is near!

Notes

1 *Terminal Identity* is the title of a fine and provocative book by Scott Bukatman (1993). His term is an apt description of my computer experience and one that resonates with the next step of the Monster's descendants on the way toward the eclipse of the human body.
2 This conjunction between the heart and the world that surrounds it happened also with the creation of the heart as a pump. It is no mere coincidence that when William Harvey published his textbook in 1628 in which he described the circulation of the blood throughout the body, the exploration of the Earth was already on its way, the minting and circulation of money was also in place, and Copernicus had already set the Earth in orbit around the sun. For a detailed description of these events and their relationships see my *Mirror and Metaphor: Images and Stories of Psychological Life* (Romanyshyn, 2001, Chapter four).
3 In her column in the Sunday Review of *The New York Times* on September 23, 2017 Maureen Dowd made a very clear statement about the dangers of the world-wide-web, specifically in her article about Mark Zuckerberg, the founder of Facebook. Her primary concern was how Facebook has become a powerful engine that can and has warped democracy. But what I find most important in her article is her comparison of Zuckerberg to Victor Frankenstein. In the context of her concerns and criticisms with regard to the role of Facebook in aiding Russian attempts to meddle in the 2016 election, she quotes *Times* columnist Kevin Roose, who calls Facebook's policies its "Frankenstein Moment." Dowd specifically compares that comment to the moment when Victor Frankenstein confesses his fears that the monster he made would be the cause of all sorts of new problems.

She is right to be concerned as *The Frankenstein Prophecies* offers a narrative about the ongoing consequences of Victor Frankenstein's fears.

Finally, referring to Elon Musk who has been critical of Zuckerberg's dreams, Dowd says that he has been "sounding the alarm for years about the danger of Silicon Valley's creations of AI mind children." These children are in fact the offspring of Victor Frankenstein's Promethean dreams of those whom he feared would bring havoc in the future for all human kind. Zuckerberg is a prophetic expression of Victor Frankenstein's dream as nightmare. He is an exemplar of the consequences of denying responsibility for one's actions. As Dowd points out, "The digerati at Facebook and Google are either being naïve or cynical and greedy in thinking that it's enough just to have a vague code of conduct that says 'Don't be evil,' as Google does."

One last point needs to be made here. As she ends her column, she points out that Zuckerberg's apparent intentions to run for president, has led to his confession that he is no longer an atheist. Is there any better connection to be made between the mind children who have created the world-wide-web and are continuing to advance its power and domination over the globe and the god like dreams of Victor Frankenstein? No longer an atheist, Mark Zuckerberg is a prototype of a new kind of god beguiled by his technological powers.
4 The computer screen is itself the prophetic amplification of Alberti's window. A detailed discussion of the historical origins of this term in the context of Alberti's work and its relation to the development of science and technology is present in *Technology as*

Symptom and Dream (Romanyshyn, 1989/2006). See also note three in Question One. Here I want to note a key difference between the TV and computer screen. With the TV screen we are exemplars of the spectator self who sees but is not seen. With the computer screen the one who sees is also seen, but as a disembodied self. At www the gap between the spectator self on this side of Alberti's window and the specimen body on the other is being dissolved into a new self on the way toward Kurzweil's Singularity where human beings transcend the body.

5   The Indo European root of explain refers to a flat land and the Latin root means level, even and spread out. So, when we ex-plain something we are, so to speak, living in a flat land and in effect erasing or at least smoothing out differences. A god that is ex-plainable is a god that has been leveled down to our plane of existence.

6   See Sherry Turkle (2011).

7   See my article "Terminal Talk: Reflections on Thinking and Saying in the Digital World" Romanyshyn (2016). In this essay I try to begin to find my way into thinking, saying and teaching in the space of the webinar. I begin to try on thinking, saying and teaching as if I were a self in space-less space and timeless time, as if I were experiencing for a moment floating in digital space without the weight of flesh, an astronaut in this new landscape of weightless existence, as if I were immortal, a glimpse of what it might be like to be eternal, like a god. Something vital to who we are is left behind as we enter the digital world and this sense of loss colors one's initial forays into this other country with a mood of sorrow. But where is a place for a mood of sorrow or for Eros in the digital world? Is the manic pace of the digital world where one can be on call 24/7 a defense against loss, a wall against sorrow?

8   The etymological roots of the word friend connect it to the Norse goddess of love, Frigg who is the wife of Odin. In this connection there is something sacred about the friend, which is watered down when it is commercialized as a measure of one's popularity. This minimalizing of the sacred is part of the ethos of the technological world we are creating in which the sacred has been eclipsed.

9   This is a riff on e. e. cummings (1926/1959, p. 29). In his poem, "voices to voices/lip to lip," his one-eyed son of a bitch is one who has invented an instrument to measure spring. From thermometers to computers, we are being measured and isolated. The poet's line anticipates Turkle's (2011) take on how we are alone together in the digital world.

10 In this film Ben Affleck plays a CPA with high functioning autism, who also happens to be engaged in criminal activity. Working outside the margins, Christian Wolff, the character played by Affleck, suggests that the medicalization of pathology in our culture marginalizes the person. We become, as it were, the labels diagnosed by the medical establishment and treated by the pharmaceutical industry.

11 *The Big Bang Theory* is a popular television program whose major character, Dr. Sheldon Cooper, is a physicist whose genius level intelligence lacks any sense of an emotional understanding of others. He is a symbol of someone who has Asperger syndrome. But his condition is displayed with such a comic sense that the continuing popularity of the program attests to the normalization of this condition that is marginalized. He is perhaps a mirror of what we are all becoming at the computer terminal where our terminal identity is a disembodied image presence. He is in a way the Monster made into a comedic figure that allows us to laugh at the image of ourselves in the mirror, thereby diminishing the anxiety of its danger. Beguiled by the laughter soundtrack, which in fact signals us when to laugh, we not only forget what is being lost in normalizing what lies outside the margins of the collective mind, we forget that we have forgotten. The monster is tamed. But at what price?

12 Kurzweil's book poses an articulate defense of the pace and goals of biogenetic and computer technologies. No one can avoid coming to terms with his work if one wishes to offer a caution about his vision.

13 Stephen Hawking actually changed his mind about the moment of singularity when he predicted that a particle of matter does escape the gravitational pull of black holes while its anti-particle falls back into it. While his view was rejected initially as nonsense, it has

proven to be correct and today that emission is called Hawking radiation. The significance for our discussion of Kurzweil is that his imaginative leaps are aligned with Hawkins's revised view. This revised view is, in fact, a key point for his claim that Hawkins's view of black holes indicates that "a universe that is well designed to create black holes would be one that is well designed to optimize its intelligence" (Kurzweil, 2005, pp. 363–364). As we shall see, this daring leap is a foundation for Kurzweil's dream of *Homo sapiens* ultimately transcending its baggage of biology. We are, as it were, destined to seed the universe with our intelligence. Indeed, it is as if our intelligence is itself a form of Hawking radiation.

Kurzweil's vision of our destiny is Descartes's dream carried into the clouds. The mind domain of Descartes, which is separate from the body domain, is a philosophical speculation that has materialized into the scientific study of the brain. The "I think" of Descartes has now become the cortex while the "I am" is rooted in the oldest part of the human brain, the heritage of our reptilian past. Descartes's dualism is an idea that now matters.

But we should pause to consider this move into the cloud, where, as we shall see later in this question, Kurzweil says we will download all human intelligence and seed the universe with all the bits and bytes of our knowledge. If we can assume that these bits and bytes of data seeds refer to the cortex level of the brain, then to the degree that we move into the cloud we increasingly leave behind a sense of ourselves that is more like our reptilian past. The increasing level of violence in our world today often sparked by images from the digital world is a harbinger of this possibility.

From Descartes's philosophical speculation through Victor Frankenstein's use of his scientific and technological power to create life to Kurzweil's Cloud(y) dream, we have been engaged in a flight from death. At the root of this denial of death, of this dream to be the death of Death, is a flight from the body. In the Cloud we will be like Angels or Spirits floating free of the animal body.

14 We have all but forgotten the work of Freud and Jung, whose view of dreams and their value went beyond Freud's. In fact, the work of depth psychology has been buried under the same materialistic spirit and utiltatarian values of the Promethean mind which reduces dreams to neurobiological explanations. As a consequence of this reductive materialism, unconscious dynamics have been dismissed, much to our peril. As Jung has noted, the hypothesis of the unconscious "is of absolutely revolutionary significance in that it could radically alter our view of the world." It would require us to acknowledge that "our view of the world can be but a provisional one" (1946/1960). See also Question Three, note 14.

Regarding the wisdom of the dream, I take up this point in Question Eight as a seed of hope in Mary Shelley's story.

15 This issue is at the heart of the Turing Test. Created by Alan Turing in 1950 this test is designed to investigate if a machine can exhibit intelligent behavior equivalent to, or indistinguishable from, that of a human. It is a harbinger of the development of Artificial Intelligence.

The film *Ex Machina* released in 2014 depicts this test. In the film a machine like human is able to convince a human being she is real. In addition, the film powerfully suggests a future where such humanoid machines are in the human world as "she" escapes from the lab where she was created. In the film *Her* released in 2013, Scarlett Johansson is Samantha, a computer-generated operating system with whom Theodore Twombly, played by Joaquin Phoenix, falls in love. The movie shows that this possibility is especially powerful for the lonely soul, which is so characteristic today when at our computer terminals we are alone, as Sherry Turkle notes in *Alone Together* (2011). *Her* is prophetic of the orphan quality of our experience in the digital world, a feminine image of the "Monster's" loneliness at the very origins of his "birth" when he, born of no mother, is abandoned by his creator father. Moreover, both films portray the prophetic descendants of Victor Frankenstein's Monster, feminine offspring that Victor Frankenstein so feared, expressions of the race of devils which he worried would be the ruination of mankind.

Kurzweil predicts that computers will pass the Turing Test, "indicating intelligence indistinguishable form that of biological humans, by the end of the 2020s" (2005, p. 25). The two films cited above have already imagined that scenario.

16 Elon Musk predicts that the technology is already available to allow us to add another layer of intelligence on the human brain. Atop the limbic system, which is the seat of our instinctual intelligence and the cortex, which is the seat of our rational intelligence, we will add a layer of digital intelligence, which will connect our brains to the World Wide Web. He even suggests that such an advance will not require invasive surgery.

17 Heidegger (1969). This distinction is fundamental to Heidegger's philosophical reflections on technology. See Question Two, note one.

18 See Jaron Lanier (2010), an insightful and important book. In the context of Kurzweil's prediction that by the end of the 2020s computers will pass the Turing Test (see note 15 above), Lanier points out that the test does not indicate if machines have become smarter or we have lowered our own standards of intelligence. Kurzweil's optimism leads Lanier to question how far our sense of personhood has degraded when we are collectively swept up in what he describes as an "illusion" (Lanier, 2010, p. 32).

This question of personhood is a key point in Question Three.

19 For a discussion of Durer and that image of an ideal nude see Romanyshyn (1989/ 2006, p. 118).

20 See Slater (2006). His essay, "Cyborgian Drift: Resistance is Not Futile," is one of the finest pieces to question the psychological consequences of our enchantment with the cyborg fantasy. The recurring appearance of the Borg in the Star Trek franchise is evidence of this mesmerizing effect that this image has upon the collective psyche.

21 Kurzweil, *The Age of Spiritual Machines* (1999). This book is a harbinger of what is to come in *The Singularity is Near* (2005). The two subtitles are a measure of Kurzweil's flight from the human. The subtitle of the earlier work is "When Computers Exceed Human Intelligence." The subtitle of the latter book is "When Humans Transcend Biology." The background of both subtitles is the Promethean leap and the shadow of Victor Frankenstein.

22 *West World* is a popular television series that plays on this theme of cyborgs turning against their makers. The series, which first aired in 2016, is set in a wild-west theme park where android hosts are programmed to be of service to wealthy visitors. Although programmed to not harm their visitors, as the series progresses the androids begin to discover who they are and proceed to go beyond their programs.

23 For Kurzweil's list of the principals involved in his notion of Singularity see Kurzweil (2005, pp. 25–29).

24 I use Don Quixote as an example here because his quest has mostly become identified with quixotic, impractical and foolish gestures. But his story is actually anything but foolish. His tilting at windmills was in service to recovering a lost tradition of chivalry. So quixotic or not perhaps we all need to have a bit of Don Quixote's respect for what is being lost as we rush toward Kurzweil's prophetic amplification of Victor Frankenstein's dream to create life.

25 In Jungian terms there is a god complex in Kurzweil's work that is not seriously examined. This was in fact the opening issue in Question One of *The Frankenstein Prophecies*. Indeed, *The Frankenstein Prophecies* is framed by Jung's psychology. Attending to the Monster's tale told on the margins of the collective mind, we encounter the shadow element of the god complex in the human psyche. This shadow element lingers today in symptomatic form explored as prophecies in each of the eight Questions. The symptom is the doorway into the archetypal patterns of Victor Frankenstein's god complex: the flight from death, the resentment of the flesh, the dying of nature, the eclipse of the sacred, the sacrifice of the feminine, an old ethic that denies the value and wisdom of the dream, and the longing for home exemplified by the figures of the orphan and the refugee.

26 Wim Wenders's 1987 film *Wings of Desire* tells the story of invisible angels who populate the city of Berlin and who can listen in on the thoughts, fantasies and worries of the

people who live there. The film focuses on two of the angels who hear the deep sense of isolation and loneliness experienced by the human beings even in the midst of the crowded city.

Wenders's movie owes much of its inspiration to the work of the poet Rainer Maria Rilke, especially his *Duino Elegies*. Indeed, this magical film is a reply to the opening lines of Rilke's poem: "Who, if I cried, would hear me among the angelic orders?" (1939, p. 21) For Wenders we are in our loneliness and isolation heard by the angelic orders. In 1987 we were on the cusp of creating the world-wide-web. How much more today in our wired-webbed-world would the angelic orders be present? We shall explore this issue in Question Six where we consider if Mary Shelley's story is a prophecy of our being homeless in the wired and webbed world.

Wenders's film also explores Rilke's poetic description of the relation between angels and us. In Rilke's cosmology the Angel is so far above us that the elegiac song of lament about this state of our being in the beginning of the poem becomes the condition for the elegies as a song of praise about us who exist in the place between the Angel and the Animal. So, even while in the First Elegy Rilke says "the knowing brutes are aware/that we don't feel very securely at home/within our interpreted world" (ibid.), the Ninth Elegy is a poetic celebration of the gap between Angel and Animal where we are to praise the world to the Angel, to tell them things. Indeed, the elegance, beauty and spiritual power of the Ninth Elegy is akin to Beethoven's "Ode to Joy," the fourth movement in his Ninth Symphony.

For Rilke, then, we have something to give, something that even the Angel might desire, and the title of Wenders's film underscores this point. Angelic wings are wings of desire, and Damiel is the angel who desires the fleshy relation that humans have with the world. What Damiel wishes is to be mortal and embodied so as to feel the bond between the sensual flesh of the body and the sensuous appeals of the world, even something so simple as holding in one's cold hands on a winter morning a hot cup of coffee. In the scenes in which Damiel is with a trapeze artist with whom he has fallen in love, the black and white field becomes filled with color. In the gap, Eros paints the world in rich hues. In addition, in the place we occupy between the angel and the animal the figure of the trapeze artist is an emblem of who we are—beings who dwell between the erotic tension of spirit and matter. She, who soars above the ground, is a symbol of that spiritual pole of humankind that is inevitably still bound to matter. She is neither pure angelic spirit nor brute, animal matter, and it is this paradox that draws the angel to her and to us.

In the context of this film and Rilke's poem, we need to wonder, then, about the psychological consequences of Kurzweil's leap into the clouds. What happens to us if and when we erase that gap that is the measure of who we are? Who are we if and when we become, as a new species of *Homo sapiens, Homo angelicus*?

As we approach Kurzweil's Singularity, it is our technological intelligence that will finally enable us to transcend our biology. *Homo angelicus* as the triumph of spirit over matter, is the triumph of the Promethean mind in which intelligence is what spirit has become in our technologically engineered world.

But do we leap even beyond Rilke's Angelic Order to become *Homo deus*?

Homo Deus: A Brief History of Tomorrow (2017) is the title of Yuval Noah Harari's sequel to his bestselling book *Sapiens: A Brief History of Humankind* (2005). More needs to be said about Harari's excellent books but that is for another time. Suffice it here to say that while I agree with his historical analysis of the development from *Homo sapiens* to *Homo deus*, I sharply differ with the absence of the dangers of that development in his work. There are no monstrous shadows in his work, which in the end reads as a materialist reduction and subsequent dehumanization of what it means to be a human being.

When he explains for example how the right hemisphere of the brain makes up stories to fill in the gap between what it fails to notice, the explanations dismiss the meaning, value and experience of what we do as story makers. He equates the condition for experience with the meanings of the experience and thus reduces the latter to the former. That is like explaining the dream through brain functioning, which ultimately leads to the dismissal of the dream and its wisdom. In this regard Harari might even be seen to be continuing the dream of Victor Frankenstein and Ray Kurzweil. For more about Harari's work see Question Three, note 14.

Finally, regarding the absence of the monstrous shadow in his analysis of our development from *Homo sapiens* to *Homo deus*, it is helpful to recall that Joyce Carol Oates titles her Afterword to Mary Shelley's story "Frankenstein's Fallen Angel." That fallen angel is the Monster and *The Frankenstein Prophecies* has been tracing out the lines of his descendants, which shadow his maker's dream. Kurzweil's enhanced humans, which I have described as *Homo angelicus*, are his fallen angels.

27 Kurzweil (2005). See pp. 30–33 for a conversation Kurzweil imagines between himself and the unenhanced humans.

28 My eldest son who has had Parkinson's disease for over twenty-five years told me a dream in which he saw he was more machine than human. He told me that he preferred being human even with Parkinson's.

29 Throughout this book I have been trying to stay attuned to the subtlety of words. How we speak and write is how we come to see the world and how we see the world is how we come to speak and write about it. There is no hyphen in Kurzweil's use of the word. Using the hyphen here for un-enhanced is meant to make us pause for a moment and call our attention to how its absence contributes to its normalization.

30 Regarding the disappearance of angels see Romanyshyn (1989/2006) and my essay "On Angels and Other Anomalies of Imaginal Life," in Romanyshyn (2002). See also Margaret Wertheim (1999).

Question Six

WWW: ADRIFT IN THE DIGITAL WORLD

Is Mary Shelley's story a prophecy of being homeless in a wired, webbed world?

The Monster's lament

John Milton's book, *Paradise Lost*, was the key for the Monster to understand his relation to his maker. He found that book during his forest wanderings after he quit Ingolstadt, the city of his unnatural birth where he was first sparked into life. Reading it as a true history, he comes to see himself as a new Adam, and, like that first man, he bewails his condition of isolation and abandonment by his god, Victor Frankenstein.

But unlike Adam the Monster knows not only that he has no Eve, but also that he is even more a solitary outcast than was Satan. As he bitterly says to his creator, Satan at least "had his companions, fellow-devils, to admire and encourage him." Continuing this comparison, he implies how his creator god is inferior to the God who made Adam. That God "made man beautiful and alluring, after his own image," while his form is a " filthy type" of his creator, which, he adds, is all the "more horrid from its very resemblance" (Shelley, 1818).

Imagine the depth of the Monster's lament! His own maker is a mirror, which not only distorts but also mocks his resemblance to him; just as all others whom he meets in his wanderings reflect this horrible and cruel difference. Are we not able to sympathize with him and understand these words he speaks to his creator? "My person was hideous, and stature gigantic: what did this mean? Who was I? What was I? Whence did I come? What was my destination?"(Shelley, 1818).

As a new Adam he is the first of his kind, but after Victor destroys the mate he promised him he believes he will also be the only and the last one of his kind. Spurned by all whom he meets, abhorred even by his maker, he says to Frankenstein, "what hope can I gather from your fellow creatures, who owe me nothing?" Vilified by all, he says his natural benevolence toward humanity sours in his utter isolation. Miserably alone, he adds, "The desert mountains and dreary glaciers are my refuge" (Shelley, 1818).

"Who was I?"

"What was I?"

What is it like to not know who or what one is, or even to have a ground for such questions?

"Whence did I come?"

"What was my destination?"

What is it like to be a being with no ancestors, with no memory of a history, and with not even some vague sense of one's direction or purpose or meaning?

Perhaps the most illustrative moment of the Monster's lamentable plight occurs in that part of Mary Shelley's story when his hopes to be accepted by the members of the De Lacey family end in devastating failure.

During one of his flights from those whom he encounters and who attack him out of their fear of his appearance, he stumbles upon a cottage whose inhabitants are De Lacey, an old blind man, his son, Felix, and his daughter Agatha. Finding a hiding place in a hovel adjacent to the cottage, he secludes himself from them, while, over the course of nearly a year during which he secretly observes their behavior and is slowly educated into their language, he learns their story. He begins to imagine them as his protectors, even as a kind of family, and to his maker he describes the cottage as "the only school in which I had studied human nature" (Shelley, 1818).

The Monster is transformed by this education and it kindles in him a hope that he might one day find in their company some respite from his isolation and loneliness. When the day finally arrives and he presents himself to the old blind man who is alone in the cottage, he tells him his story.

"I am an unfortunate and deserted creature; I look around, and I have no relation or friend upon earth."

"To be friendless is indeed to be unfortunate," the old man replies.

Encouraged by this sign of compassion, the Monster proclaims, "You raise me from the dust ... and I trust that I shall not be driven from the society and sympathy of your fellow-creatures." Continuing with this sense of hope, he says, "How can I thank you, my best and only benefactor? From your lips first have I heard the voice of kindness directed towards me" (Shelley, 1818).

The old blind man listens to the Monster and, thus, is not blind to who he is by his disfigured image. If we can get past the images of Victor's Monster that have haunted the collective mind, then perhaps we can feel the Monster's sense of hope and see him for who he is. His words might even elicit from us some kindness and compassion for him, as they do with the old man who says to him, "I am blind, and cannot judge of your countenance, but there is something in your words which persuades me you are sincere" (Shelley, 1818).

But that is not the story that has been told by Mary Shelley,[1] and while the old man's blindness allows him to "see" the Monster through his words, his children do not see him as the old blind man does. When Felix and Agatha return to the cottage, they are horrified by the Monster's hideous form. Felix and Agatha are blind in another way. Their blindness is not a physical matter. It is rather a blindness of the heart, a psychological blindness, which mimics our own blindness to what is "other," to what is different from us and judged monstrous by that standard. And so, with curses thrown at the Monster and sticks to beat him, Felix drives him from the cottage into a deeper exile that is beyond hope. Never to see the De Lacey's again, the Monster says to Frankenstein that their absence has "broken the only link that held me to the world" (Shelley, 1818).

Of orphans and refugees

Telling Victor Frankenstein his experience, the Monster is telling us his side of the story. His lament is a tale of one who is beyond the pale, a tale told by an outcast who is outside the community of human kind. It is a tale from the margins of one who epitomizes the orphan. It is a tale of his exile and wandering as a refugee.

In Mary Shelley's story there are moments when the Monster understands himself to be an orphan or a refugee. After he flees from his unhallowed birthplace in Ingolstadt and starts his wanderings, he begins to understand he "possessed no money, no friends, no kind of property." In his flight, "I saw and heard of no one like me," and this awareness leads him to ask himself if he is the very thing his maker has called him, a "monster, a blot upon the earth." As such, he realizes he would be one from whom "all men fled, and whom all men disowned" (Shelley, 1818). Looking back he knows the causes of this fate and says to his maker, "No father has watched my infant days, no mother had blessed me with smiles and caresses." He then adds that throughout his life he has never "seen a being resembling me, or who claimed any intercourse with me" (Shelley, 1818).

As one reads Mary Shelley's story, passages like these make one pause. In these passages we do have some of the Monster's side of the Frankenstein story. His unnatural birth, the hideous form of his appearance, his abandonment by his maker, have made him a refugee. But, given these same circumstances, he is and has been also an orphan since the very first moment of his conception in the mind of Victor Frankenstein.

And yet this side of the story, the Monster's tale as orphan and refugee, is largely ignored, and essentially untold. His maker's story, the one that Victor Frankenstein relates to Captain Walton, has claimed the day, while the Monster with his tale waits in exile on the margins.

To understand the Monster's tale of being an orphan and a refugee, and to bring out the kinship between these two patterns as well as their differences, a story wants a story. Here is one of an orphan and a refugee, my father's story of his father and mother.

The falling star

My father had been gone for some time. Drafted into some army soon after we had arrived from New York in 1914, he went away to fight in a war. Why my father and mother had left our home and had taken my older brother and me to this other country, I did not know. I had only heard whispers about having to sell some land because his relatives had written to him and told him that a war was coming.

I was afraid a lot at first. The words were strange and there was no one with whom I could say the words I knew. I had no friends and so little seemed familiar to me. I felt many times like a stranger.

There was a camp of some sort close by the farmhouse where we were living, and on occasion I could hear men signing songs that sounded so sad. But I could not understand the language. I was told they were Russian prisoners and that their songs were about feeling so far from home and that singing them was a way to remember home. But I still felt sad as I would listen and wonder if they would ever go home again. In such moments I wished my father would come back and take us home. But he never did.

Even though my father was gone, I had my mother. But I did worry what would happen to me if she were gone, especially because she had been sick for a while.

When my mother started to get very ill, I would go to a field near the house and lie on my back in the grass to look at the early evening sky and the stars as they began to appear. The warmth of the sun that still lingered in the field and the sweet smell of the hay made me feel safe. Sometimes I could feel myself becoming sleepy.

One time while I was watching the stars something happened that I have never forgotten. Nor did I tell this story to anyone because I did not have words to say what I saw and how I understood what had happened to me that night. But I tell the story to you so that it will not be forgotten.

As I lay there in the soft grass, as the sun was beginning to set and the stars began to fill the sky above me, one stood out because of its brightness. As it grew brighter the star became bigger. Slowly at first but then very fast, it seemed to be moving across the sky and falling toward the field. At first I was amazed. A star was falling from the sky, and as I watched it fall its brightness began to fade. But then I became afraid. Even to this day I do not understand how as I watched the falling star I knew my mother was dying.

I ran to the house, running away as much from what I knew as I was running toward home to see her. But as fast as I could run it was not then fast enough to run from what I knew. And as I tell my story now that star is still falling and I am still running.

The star had fallen and my mother was dead. I was eight years old, an immigrant in a foreign land, without a father and without a mother. The home that I once had was gone. I was now an orphan.

Unwanted, often hungry and cold and often ill treated, my brother and I were passed back and forth among relatives in the war ravished landscapes of the Ukraine. Nine years after the star had fallen, my brother and I were returned to New York. Coming home we were processed at Ellis Island as refugees.

Orphans and refugees are similar insofar as both are homeless in their own particular way. Each is without a place, each lives in exile as marginal people, gypsies in the general sense of that word, wanderers, drifters and forever on the way from nowhere to nowhere.

But, while similar they are not identical. An orphan is a refugee but a refugee is not necessarily or always an orphan. A refugee might have a home place that is or has been lost, while the orphan has a more tenuous sense of home, which gives one a sense of belonging. Ulysses, for example, is a refugee of the Trojan wars trying to find his way home, but he is not an orphan. In his wanderings he has kin, is one of a tribe of warriors and has a tradition that guides his actions. The orphan not only has none of these ties, he or she is more often than not haunted by a lingering obsession about his or her origins.

An orphan is a specific state of being. It is a dimension of one's identity, like being, for example, an identical twin. As a state of being, orphan is as much a mark of one's psychological traits as genetic markers are of one's biological traits. Orphan, we might say, is a component of one's psychological character.[2]

A refugee on the other hand is a condition one is thrown into by circumstances that uproot one from one's place. One is made into a refugee in response to forces of oppression that compel one to flee, displaced like refugees of wars, economic crises and current effects of climate change.

But in spite of these differences, the orphan and the refugee in their shared sense of homelessness are kin of the Monster. Orphan and refugee are guises in which the Monster haunts the margins of the collective mind. They are the feared prophetic offspring of Victor Frankenstein's dream of being a new god, which we continue to create and exile to the margins of invisibility.

Frankenstein as Prophecy

Globalization

In the interest of expanded and free trade policies, the proponents of globalization have since the 1990s celebrated a vision of a world where barriers and borders would fade away. It has not quite worked out as it was imagined, as the economic crises in the European Union have shown. In addition, the dream of a world without borders has produced unintended consequences as ruinous economic policies have been exacerbated by wars and climate crises, which have created an overwhelming number of refugees. Initially welcomed by a number of countries in the EU, restrictive policies have followed, which have seen the rise of political parties with nationalistic agendas. While global economic policies, wars and climate crises have created refugees, they have been increasingly demonized as walls are built to keep them away. The drumbeat in the United States to build a wall on its southern border illustrates the dangerous practice of scapegoating the "Other," of turning the "Other" into an enemy, as a means of furthering one's own agendas. Refugees created by these crises have become the monsters we have made.

The dream of a world without borders has an ironic side because such a world does exist within our world of walls and refugees: the world-wide-web breaks down barriers and borders. Indeed, while walls are being built, the web is creating resistance to as well as support for them. Regardless of which side of the wall one stands, the human tragedy is available 24/7 and worldwide for all to see and experience. On television, in newspapers and especially on the web, the faces of those displaced seep through the barriers of denial. Perhaps it is the face of one of those many children who stare back at us with their haunted and nearly empty eyes. Their world has been so shattered that we might well wonder if the stars are continuing to fall from the sky.

Whom are we looking at when we look into their faces?

Do refugees mirror not just the monstrous side of Victor Frankenstein's god face but also show us the dark image of our own god like dreams?

In the faces of those on the road in exile and in the faces of the homeless and jobless on the margins, perhaps we catch a glimpse of the sacred depth of human life that has been masked by the monstrous beliefs in our god like powers.

Is it on the road and on the margins that the journey of homecoming begins?

But it is difficult to look in the mirror and not be blind to all except what we wish to see and need to be. We prefer the fairy tale:

> Mirror, Mirror on the wall,
> Who's the fairest of them all?[3]

Going blind

In the spring of 1999 I was preparing a short video on the conflict in Kosovo to present at a conference on war and violence. The war, which had begun in February 1998, was marked by numerous atrocities bordering on genocide and for the conference I wanted to move beyond the usual academic format of a paper. I wanted to bring that conflict into the room to capture something of the visceral sense of its horror. I was hoping to move the war and its atrocities from the head to the heart, to embody the spoken word with a feeling response, to awaken the imagination to war. Photographing a number of images that appeared daily in newspapers and periodicals, I had prepared some music to accompany the display of those images and had written brief comments to use periodically during the presentation.

Even today as I write the words above, I realize that I had no conscious awareness of what was motivating me to move well beyond my familiar and comfortable style to attempt this project. But, as I look back now I am reconnected with who I was then, one who had just published in 1999 a memoir of an unexpected death of a loved one suffered seven years earlier, which uprooted me and brought me face to face with the experience of loss.[4]

That year marked a radical shift in my life and work as the outer events of the Kosovo war and the inner events of my life converged toward the theme of loss and its accompanying images of homelessness, exile and homecoming. In this reciprocity between inner life and outer events, the supposed fixed boundary between the private realms of experience and the public realms of events proved to be a permeable membrane. The events of that conflict were drawing me out of myself toward them and I was being called toward them because I was akin to them. I was being addressed by the events, being educated into a way of being impregnated by them through the ear, present and responsive to them in this intimate manner compared with knowing about them from the distance of that spectator mind whose eye, as we have seen, takes the measure of the world from afar.

That fateful year of 1999 also marked a turning toward this book, a turning to that marginal work where what we have exiled to the margins becomes, like Victor Frankenstein's Monster, monstrous. The images of the atrocities of war were monstrous to me, unbearable, foreign, strange, and I was stumbling blindly into them even as I wished and had heretofore managed to turn a blind eye toward them. But the voice of the images on the margins of mind was irresistible. The eyes of loss and sorrow and fear and hopelessness on the faces of the many refugees of the war shone in the darkness of the video room where I was working with the images and music. A line of men walking on a road toward some unseen destiny was itself already intolerable, but when I noticed the look of one of those men holding the hand of a young child, perhaps his son, his eyes spoke an appeal that felt immediately directed to me. It was impossible to refuse that look but it was too much to bear, and in that moment as I was splicing that image into place I went blind in the upper left quadrant of my left eye.

Blind to the refugees that our wars have created, I was blindsided by the refugees of that war. Blindsided by the economic policies of corporate global greed so intimately connected to such wars, are we blind to the refugees created by them?

Marginal work is blood work, a way of working that matters to the heart. It is a work of the embodied mind, a way of making the ideas we think and the words we say a matter of flesh. Moving to the margins to think in response to what addresses us from that place is a different way of knowing. It is a way of moving beyond knowing about something to becoming a part of what one knows.

Victor Frankenstein, as we have seen, is never moved or touched by the words of the Monster he made. Like the old blind man De Lacey, Victor Frankenstein is also blind. But his blindness is not an anatomical condition. Rather, Victor Frankenstein is blinded by his dream of being a new creator god and in that blindness he does not see the being he has made. And, when it is no longer possible for him to remain blind, when he first does see that the thing he made does not conform to his dream, he labels his creation Monster, grows deaf to all *its* appeals to assuage *its* suffering and loneliness, and condemns *it* to perpetual exile.[5]

Nameless as he is, Victor Frankenstein's Monster is also anonymous, an *It* whose impersonal status makes his presence even more alarming. In this regard the nightmare side of Frankenstein's god like dream appears today in the guise of stateless terrorists who are not bounded by familiar borders. The fear they strike in us is that they can be anywhere and everywhere.

What's in a name? Terrorist and refugee are different ways in which the story of Victor Frankenstein and his Monster live on today as prophecies. One is stateless and the other homeless, and while the terrorists are identified and hunted, much like Victor Frankenstein pursued his Monster to kill him, the refugee remains more or less unnamed, like Frankenstein's nameless Monster has since his birth.

The three-year-old child who washed ashore on a beach in Turkey in September 2015 after drowning in the Mediterranean Sea, just one of countless refugee children and adults made homeless by the war in Syria, is a searing image of exile. But he had a name: Alan Kurdi!

Knowing his name, the global category of refugee becomes an individual story.

Knowing his name, the impersonal becomes personal.

Knowing his name, he perhaps redeems something for Victor Frankenstein's Monster. He becomes perhaps one of those children that Victor Frankenstein feared would be born of his Monster and the mate he had desired, and thus that small child might open our eyes to the very real danger of our god like Promethean dreams to remake the world in our own image.

Terrorists and refugees! Who is in a name does matter, because what is in a name is a story, a dream, and maybe a prophecy.

Refugee!

In 1914 the term was applied to civilians in Flanders who were heading west to escape the blood bath of World War I. That war has never really ended. It is estimated that today there are some 65 million refugees worldwide, people forced from their homes by economic, political and environmental crises.[6]

Sixty-five million refugees!

Sixty-five million homeless people in exile!

The numbers are staggering and increasing. The United Nations refugee agency estimates that extreme weather events displace over 20 million people each year. In the context of this global human tragedy, we can no longer ask for whom the bell tolls, because it tolls for all of us.[7]

Estranged from nature

There is a moment in Mary Shelley's story when Victor Frankenstein realizes what his dream to become a new creator god has cost him. Telling his story to Captain Walton, he confesses that in service to his dream to "renew life where death had apparently devoted the body to corruption ... I pursued nature to her hiding places ... and lost all soul or sensation but for this one pursuit." As he continues, he seems to acknowledge what his single minded pursuit exacted from him, adding that while he shut himself in his "solitary chamber, or rather cell ... my workshop of filthy creation," the summer that passed "was a beautiful season; never did the fields bestow a more plentiful harvest, or the vines yield a more luxuriant vintage." And, then, in the context of these words, he concludes with the rueful remark, "but my eyes were insensible to the charms of nature" (Shelley, 1818).

When the charms of nature no longer inspire us, when nature has become so measured and mapped that its capacity to enchant the imagination has withered, do we begin to sense that we are homeless, without any roots, sensing however vaguely a feeling of being nowhere in the negative utopia of an un-world created by the Promethean mind dramatically personified in Victor Frankenstein?

Is our insensitivity toward nature, our indifference to it as anything but a resource for our willful abuse, a first step toward becoming orphans in the deepest and most profound sense of that term, human beings whose god like dream to become our own creators has broken the ties between us and the natural world?

Victor Frankenstein is a man who has cut himself off from the seasons and rhythms of nature. Ironically Victor's Monster is the very opposite of his maker for the rhythms of nature are what initially awaken him to himself. Is the Monster on the margins the one who might know the way back?

From pole to pole

In Question Two I used the image of the melting polar ice to show how Mary Shelley's story might be a prophecy of the dying of nature as we have come to know it. But I also said that when I traveled to the Antarctic in 2009, I was deeply moved by its majestic landscape. Mary Shelley's story ends at the other polar extreme of the Arctic. It is there that the Monster and his maker bring their struggle to its conclusion. But while her story ends there, the tale of Victor Frankenstein and his Monster is not finished. Indeed, it is because their tale endures that I traveled a few years after my Antarctic trip to the Arctic. The melting polar ice has a fascination. It is a crisis and an opportunity to discover perhaps in the frozen ice fields something of what we have lost.

The Antarctic is a place of majesty and beauty, its ice sculptures a kind of crystal cathedral of sacred silence and splendid solitude where I had the sense of what nature once might have been before the word.

The world before the word!

The vast whiteness of that place is more than a geographical location. It is also a landscape of the imagination, which haunts the human heart and awakens a dim remembrance of a time when mind and nature were one. Indeed, the charm or spell of that place is that one dissolves into the landscape. One is the snow, and the ice, the wind and the night. One becomes elemental and, becoming elemental for brief moments, one discovers a longing to belong again, a longing to return to what once was and still is, the longing of the orphan in all of us to come home. Such moments were tinged with irony: in that landscape so far from home, in that place at the end of the world, I felt I was starting on a journey of homecoming.[8]

This longing for home is essentially not a matter of mind. It is heartfelt. As such its displays belong more to the domain of images and feelings than the domain of ideas or reasons. They might show themselves, for example, as feelings of loneliness, of being lost, and perhaps are even to be found in the basement of one's sense of boredom or anxiety. They might also be found in one's fantasies of having once had a twin who has been lost, forgotten, left behind, or in fantasies of being adopted and having a special, unique destiny. Or, this sense of a home that has been lost might show itself in those seemingly odd attractions to other times or places where one senses having had another life. This desire to go home is also present in one's dreams, which, beyond all systems of interpretation, are matters of homework.[9]

These displays of the orphan's longing to go home are more than personal. They also percolate below the surface in the collective mind. They are, for example, the stuff of so many of our mythologies and epics as well as the stuff of films. Steven Spielberg's masterpiece *ET* is a good example.[10] It shows that as a matter of the heart this journey of homecoming has a magical quality that defies the physical, logical paradigms of mind. Eliot, the young boy who so deeply connects with the ET, is an example of this magical quality of the film, which stirs the depths of the imagination before it reaches the surface of mind. Through him we sense that a different quality of consciousness is required to go home, the sensibility of wonder and openness. In addition, through the figure of ET, who as a cosmic being is marginal to the human mind, the Monster on the margins of mind does seem to be the one who knows the way home. When ET says to Eliot, "ET, phone home" the elemental longing for home, the orphan's song that we share, is stirred to life in us, even at the risk of some slight embarrassment to be so touched by this appeal.

Homecoming!

As I write this word I am aware of another quality that haunts this longing for home. It is a mood of melancholy that characterizes the orphan, a mood that colors one's experience in shades of blue. Shades of blue like the ice that I saw when I had climbed the Franz Josef Glacier in New Zealand in 2007 and was told by the guide that blue ice is the oldest ice, the color of glacier ice when most of the air bubbles have been squeezed from it. In the Antarctic two years later, I remembered that story and wondered if blue ice is the color and mood of the ice as it falls deeper into its sleep and its breath—its anima—slows. I wondered if ice dreams and if it does what it dreams about.

Among the crystal cathedrals of the Antarctic ice I found myself so draped in the mood of melancholy and enchanted by dreams of homecoming, I wondered at times if as orphan I was dreaming those dreams or being dreamed by the ice.

But the dream of longing to go home belongs neither to us nor to nature herself. Inscribed within the human heart, this longing lies in the heart of nature as well. If nature awakens in us the longing to go home, it is because through us the *Anima Mundi*, the living soul of the world, awakens to its own longing of home, just as if we awaken Nature's longing to go home, it is because through her it quickens into life our own longing to go home.

Victor's Monster has no place in the world and homeless he has no resting place within himself.

Apart from nature the human heart is lonely!

Without us is the heart of nature also lonely?

Beyond reason, deeper than logic, the dream to go home is a dream of completing who and what we are: beings who are part of nature and not apart from it. Going home is a work of fulfilling the destiny of being a human being, of practicing homecoming as a creative act that regards home as that first and last place. On the personal level, home is that place from where we begin the day and to which we return to complete it. On the collective level, we are all dust and to dust we shall return. We are all Adam shaped from clay, born from the soil and the grave our final home.

In this regard, home is not just a house. As first and last among all places, home as a physical space is primarily an image of a sheltering place whose foundation rests upon the earth, whose roof rises toward the sky and whose walls mark that primordial boundary of the outside and the inside, that boundary of home as a temple whose threshold is the boundary between the profane and the sacred.

To be homeless then is to live life without any sense of the sacred.

To know one is an orphan is to begin the journey of homecoming as a journey toward the sacred.

If, as some have said, the gods of old have fled, have they fled to the polar regions of the world?[11]

Are they sleeping in those crystal cathedrals of ice?

Is the ecological crisis of the melting polar ice fields the gods of old awakening to reclaim their place?

Victor Frankenstein would scoff at such questions. He would remind us that he would be the new god whose creation would finally banish to the dustbin of history the gods of old born in superstition and ignorance of the laws of nature. He reminds us that he would create "A new species (that) would bless me as its creator and source; many happy and excellent natures would owe their being to me" (Shelley, 1818).

The Monster, however, tells a different tale. He waits in the Arctic night to remind us of the gods we have lost, and to resurrect in us the longing for the sacred that his maker disregarded in his creation of him.

The melting polar ice is a crisis. It is a danger but where the danger lies there is also the saving grace.[12]

The Monster on the margins is the saving grace, if we, unlike his creator god, listen to his tale. If we do so, then perhaps we might see that the grace of the melting polar ice is that it reminds us of what we are losing, the sense of the sacred as what sets a boundary to the human condition, a sense of the sacred that is a limit to the hubris of the Promethean mind. If we can see the grace in the melting polar ice, we then might see the radiance of the gods that in their absence nevertheless shine through the presence of a technological world engineered in our own image.

The polar regions of the world are the proverbial canary in the coalmine. But it is perhaps too far away not only geographically but also emotionally to stir within us some dim memory of a lost sense of the sacred and with it some hint that we are not so securely at home in our technologically engineered world. There are, however, more immediate places that might stir such memories.

Corporate places and digital spaces

We are living in strange times when local places and their customs are becoming corporatized. For example, the old neighborhood grocery stores, which one can still see in rural villages, have become quasi museum settings decked out with their antique furnishings designed to attract tourists for trips down memory lane. They are fabrications, of course, with little of the living spirit of the originals.

While such settings of bygone days drip with nostalgic sentimentality, their appeal does point to experiences which, having been lost, still linger, perhaps because they are essential to forging a feeling of community. Local taverns and coffee shops, for example, are places where one can hang out. They are places where one can meet and talk face to face with members of one's own tribe as it were, places for gossip and conversation that make a place for a cast of colorful characters. Crossing its threshold, one is neither at home nor at work, but in a third kind of place where, feeling at home among friends and companions, one can rest for an hour or two.[13]

In such places, there are masters, as it were, who know how to nurse a drink or a cup of coffee for the duration and who appreciate the restorative value of wasting time. One is not just a customer in such places. On the contrary, one is participating with others in telling stories that weave together part of the fabric of a community.

What essentially defines such places is that they are local in the sense that they are within walking distance of one's home. Indeed, part of the charm of such places is the ritual of "taking a break" by ambling down to the neighborhood coffee shop or tavern. Their locality in local space makes the "going there" part of the "being there." The amble, the stroll, can feel like an adventure. Who might one meet on the way? Who might be already there to welcome you and even cheer you across the threshold?[14]

Corporate coffee shops and bookstores and even high tech wine bars invite and foster a much different kind of experience. Corporate places, like Starbucks, for example, are digital spaces where one's consciousness, which, as embodied is always local and tribal, like all politics is essentially local, is wired into the global net. Whether or not one taps into the digital space, one is webbed in it, and the irony of such a place is that you can go there to get away from there to go everywhere and anywhere. When you get to such a corporate place the there you get to is not there, and the you who goes there is a presence that can be absent.

A laptop on the table with earplugs inserted, the art of conversation fades away, its absence hardly noticed, as the ambient background programmed music fills the empty space with an upbeat sense of optimism. In such a place one is more or less isolated. Indeed, it is as if one is in a cell, in a private space that is not, however a place of solitude.

Time for solitude is indispensible for being with others, for in solitude one learns to be with oneself, which is the other side of being with others. In solitude one has the opportunity to discover how silence is the other side of conversation. But in one's digital cell with one's cell phone nearby not only does the art of conversation fade away, solitude gives way to the illusion of being connected even as one is alone.

Have we lost the capacity to hear what is unsaid on the margins of our talk, so much of which seems, especially in these places, a kind of version of corporate speak, awash as it is in opinions and submerged in idle chatter?

Are corporate places in digital spaces the triumph of commerce over conversation?[15]

The irony here is that we hardly, if at all, notice the irony. Seduced by these ubiquitous standardized corporate places, these nowhere places that seem to be everywhere give the illusion of familiarity, and keep in place a shared fantasy that nothing has changed and that all is as it should be. These corporate places that are gateways to digital spaces, thresholds to that strange sense of place that is no place, even begin to feel normal because, as some have argued, we reached a tipping point in 2016 when "a critical mass of our lives and work had shifted away from the terrestrial world to a realm known as 'cyberspace'" (Freidman, 2017). Moreover, perhaps even more ironic than this seeming sense of digital space as the new real is that these negative U-topic places even seem utopian, like shopping malls do in their glitz, polish and sparkle and their allure of abundant treasures.

Who or what are we when we have lost the art of conversation with its demands to listen and be with the other and feel comfortable and even enjoy the slow pace of that art as one drifts with the current of what is said and remains to be said, when words have not yet become talking points?

It would not at all be just to suggest that we are refugees or orphans in these places and spaces. The gap of privilege is much too wide. And yet, that gap itself hides a danger because its privilege conceals the radical sense of alienation from being at home in the world with others in the intimacy of our embodied presence to each other. In such corporate places and digital spaces we are comfortably homeless, unknowingly oblivious and insensitive to others, anonymous persons without community who have contributed to our own sense of alienation as we drift along blissfully contented in the digital ocean. In such corporate places and digital spaces the Monster has become tamed, normalized, webbed, assimilated and silenced.

A backward glance: Earth from outer space

As we have seen, *Homo astronauticus* is the first of our kind to take leave of Earth. In that leap into space we have broken not only the physical bond of gravity between body and earth, we have also broken our psychological ties to earth as home. Ties that bind are terms whose Latin roots lead back to "*ligare,*" which gives us the word religion. The first moment of liftoff, then, is the moment when we, as *Homo astronauticus*, declare that we are no longer connected to or bound by something beyond us. It is the moment when Victor Frankenstein's dream to be a new god of creation, shatters the sacred, spiritual bond of gravity between us and earth. Free floating we enter the cosmos as wanderers in search of home, *Homo astronauticus* is an orphan.

And yet that leap into space sharpens the sense of being an orphan. It is a moment when the issue of not being at home in the technological world shines out in the interstellar night. Earthrise as seen from the moon is an image that poses two questions:

Is it a harbinger of a final farewell?

Is it a reminder of what we are leaving behind, an image that calls us not to forget?

Of course, neither one is fixed in stone. Each question testifies only to the power we have to break the native bond of gravity and escape the gravity pull of earth as home. What we do with that power, how we take it up, sets the path.

The Frankenstein Prophecies shows us the path that led to the moment of liftoff. It follows the steps that have led from Victor Frankenstein's dream to the moon and beyond. It is a path of prophecy, which, as we become aware of it, might change a fate that feels inevitable into a possibility that can be re-imagined. But for that change to happen we need to attend to the margins along the path and listen to the untold tale in Mary Shelley's story. We need to lend an ear to the whispers of the Monster on the margins and hear his tale that is the other side of his maker's dream.

The Monster in moonlight

As we move toward the margins let us return to the moon and its light. There is that moment in Mary Shelley's story when the Monster is watching Victor Frankenstein create the mate he promised to him. For the first time in his miserable existence, he has hope. She will be a companion to assuage his loneliness. Looking at her through a window, the moon shines its light on her. But Victor also sees her in moonlight. We know what is about to happen. But in those few seconds before he tears her to pieces in front of the Monster, we can imagine catching a glimpse of the Monster's face in the light of the moon.

Do we see in that soft light, so different from the light of the solar mind of his maker, the beauty of the Monster, that terrible kind of beauty of Rilke's Angel?[16]

Perhaps, if we can stand the journey, the path to the margins is a path not only to our Monsters but also to our Angels. Rilke's Angel is not, however, Kurzweil's angel. To understand the difference we have to follow a different path than the one taken by Ray Kurzweil following in the footsteps of Victor Frankenstein. This other path leads to some seeds of hope to be found in the Monster's tale, the largely untold tale in Mary Shelley's story.

Notes

1 Stories have a magical quality about them and when one is listening to a story, as one might do around a fire on a cold evening as Mary Shelley, her husband Percy and Lord Byron did that fateful night that gave birth to Frankenstein, the story being spoken opens in its listeners other stories.

Stories are the threads that weave the garment of one's life, and some of those threads appear and reappear, which give the garment its shape and style and which make up a part of the pattern of one's work. The story told in this book is one that deeply informed a primary pattern of my life and work. Indeed, that story has figured prominently in my interest in Mary Shelley's story, because it awakened in me themes of exile and homecoming and seeded my imagination with images of these themes. Stories that work in this way are gifts that if opened and not returned continue to give. They function as guides, as pole stars that lead one along a path, which one has not so much chosen as found. Indeed, I did not so much choose Mary Shelley's story as it chose me; I have not so much elected Victor Frankenstein and his Monster as companions along the way, as they elected me.

2 See Bonnie Bright (2015), whose essay is a beautiful discussion of the issue of exile and homecoming within the context of Homer's *Odyssey*. See also Bright (2012). In addition, see Kerry Ragain (2006), for an exploration of the connections between being adopted and the figure of the orphan in the archetypal background of that process.

In my therapy practice over the years, I have seen how the figure of the Orphan often appears in dreams and in fantasies of being a twin who was somehow left behind, lost or forgotten. I have come to understand that the Orphan figure refers to the twin of oneself, that one who remembers one's calling, who is, as it were, a guide, companion, perhaps even the psychological emblem of what has been called in a religious context one's guardian angel. The archetypal Orphan as a pole star that leads one home.

3 The words are from the fairytale "Snow White." In *Civilization and Its Discontents* (1930), Freud states that the meaning of evolution is to be found in the struggle between Eros as the instinct of life and Thanatos as the instinct of destruction. He then adds that "it is this battle of the giants that our nurse-maids try to appease with their lullaby about Heaven" (p. 122). Quite apart from the context of his words, Freud, a master at un-masking the delusions of life, is attesting to the enormous difficulty of facing the depths of psychological life, of making a place for the monsters we have made in our acts of denial.

4 Romanyshyn (1999).

5 For Victor Frankenstein the Monster he has made is a thing, a thing with no name and never to be seen in any other way. But the essential point of *The Frankenstein Prophecies* is to see the Monster in another way, as a being with his own agency whose tale is told from the margins, from his place of exile. Thus, the importance of attending to the words that are used in this book. Hence italics for the Monster as Victor Frankenstein sees him as an It, which keeps the Monster silenced behind the wall that has been made of his maker's denial of his responsibility toward his creation, a blind god who rails against his creation.

6 See Bonnie Bright (2012). Her essay is an insightful exploration of the issue of migration that sets the discussion within the contexts of leaving home and losing home.

7 The reference is to John Donne. The words were originally not written as a poem but as *Meditation 17 of Devotions Upon Emergent Occasions*, in 1624. Be that as it may, the words echo in our hearts as a reminder of the constant presence of death in human life. It is a bell whose ringing sound Victor Frankenstein tried to silence.

8 See Fariba Mansouri (2010), for a creative analysis of the issue of exile and homecoming in the context of an imaginal dialogue between the poet Rumi and the psychologist Carl Jung. *Encounters at the End of the World*, a 2007 documentary film by Werner Herzog tells the stories of those who are attracted to work in the Antarctic. One of the features that stands out is how many of the individuals are people who choose to live on the margins of society. Watching the film many times it is easy to see the connection between such marginal individuals and the Antarctic landscape as a landscape of homecoming.

9 The dream that took me to the Antarctic in 2009 had occurred thirty years earlier, and as I recollect those thirty years I realize that that dream and that journey also led me to Mary Shelley's story. The outer journey to the Antarctic continues in this inner journey of the imagination to the Arctic of Mary Shelley's story.

10 *ET The Extra-Terrestrial* was released in 1982 to wide acclaim. Another classic film with the same enduring theme of longing for home is *The Wizard of Oz*, released in 1939. Who would not wish for a yellow brick road to follow when such longings emerge? Mythological stories of wandering and homecoming are embedded in the western psyche in Homer's *Illiad* and *Odyssey*, in the epic story of *Gilgamesh* and in Dante's *Divine Comedy*, which describes the soul's journey of homecoming.

11 In his essay "What are Poets For?" Martin Heidegger (1950/1975) writes: "The default of God means that no god any longer gathers men and things unto himself, visibly and unequivocally, and by such gathering disposes the world's history and man's sojourn in it. The default of God forebodes something even grimmer. Not only have the gods and the god fled, but the divine radiance has become extinguished in the world's history" (p. 91; POETRY, LANGUAGE, THOUGHT by MARTIN HEIDEGGER. Translations and Introduction by Albert Hofstadter. Copyright (c) 1971 by Martin Heidegger. Courtesy of HarperCollins Publishers). Carl Jung speaks to the same concern but he tells us where the gods and the god now dwell: "The *gods have become diseases*; Zeus no longer rules Olympus but rather the solar plexus, and produces curious specimens for the doctor's consulting room, or *disorders* the brains of politicians and journalists who unwittingly let loose psychic epidemics on the world" (1957/1967).

    As *The Frankenstein Prophecies* emphasizes the Monster as outcast has returned in the guise of our collective symptoms. In these guises the Monster as the dark side of Victor Frankenstein's god complex is the return of the gods.

12 See Heidegger (1955/1977). These words about danger and grace refer to Heidegger's essay, "The Question Concerning Technology." In that essay he ascribes the danger of technology not to its machines or practices, but to the ways in which it impacts the essence of humanity, or, in Jungian terms, the soul of humanity. As such, technology is a way of framing the world and our place within it in which, failing to hear it as a claim addressed to us, we take up the powers and abilities of technology as lords of the earth. Victor Frankenstein is an emblem of Heidegger's precise understanding of technology. If one takes the time to hang around with Victor's Monster and listen to his side of the story, then one has a powerful image of Heidegger's concern. Indeed, the Monster's disfigured and scarred form is an image of how technology impacts the essence of humanity.

    I would add here that after so many years of reflecting on this question of technology guided by Heidegger's thinking, I realized the need to make his concerns about technology more accessible to the general and concerned reader, since a feeling of dread and of not being at home in a technologically fashioned world are an atmosphere around all of us and nature. Hence, *The Frankenstein Prophecies*. The actual words used by Heidegger in his essay about danger and grace are taken from the poet Holderlin: "But where danger is, grows/ The saving power also" (p. 28).

13 See Oldenburg (1989). His book, *The Great Good Place* is a delightful read that stirs the memory of places that once were integral to the sense of community. One reads it and knows in his or her bones what has been lost with the increasing dominance of corporate places.

14 *Cheers* was a very popular television sitcom that ran from 1982 to 1993. Its hold on its audience was rooted in the familiar place where a cast of odd-ball characters would settle in for talk and drink on the way home. It was a place where, as the theme song said, everybody knows your name. Now in perpetual re-runs, what once was a place where a longing for home could be assuaged for a moment or two has become a retreat into nostalgia. In such great, good places where we could meet as one who is part of a community, we are now re-made as consumers in corporate spaces.

15 See Turkle (2015).

16 For the power of the Angel as a terrible kind of beauty see Rilke's *Duino Elegies*. In The First Elegy he says, "For Beauty's nothing/but beginning of Terror we're still just able to bear" and then a few lines later adds, "Each single Angel is terrible" (1939, p. 21). I would also add here that it is the Monster in moonlight whose hopeful gaze breaks Victor Frankenstein's spectator solar mind on this side of the window. Today it is the monsters we have made in Frankenstein's wake who are breaking down the walls as they rise up on the margins of that spectator mind.

Question Seven

WHO IS THE MONSTER?

Is Mary Shelley's story a prophecy of a radical ethics?

The Monster's unspoken question

"Am I to be thought the only criminal, when all human kind sinned against me?" (Shelley, 1818). The soil in which a question grows is the dark ground that already contains some seeds of knowledge that seem otherwise unknown or have heretofore been unspoken. When the Monster asks Captain Walton this question does he already intuitively know something about himself and his maker? Does he already suspect that their relationship has been so unbalanced and tilted in favor of his creator that he has been the one and the only one of the two of them who has been regarded as a monster? The seed of knowledge in this question is fundamental to the untold tale that he carries about himself and Victor Frankenstein. Hidden in that seed of knowledge is the wisdom of this deeper question: "Who is the Monster?"

This question is a turning point in Mary Shelley's story, a place where the untold tale in her story turns toward a prophecy of another kind of ethics. The turn is a radical one that goes to the root of ignorance in our ways of knowing, roots that reach deeply into the Socratic maxim to know thyself and branch out toward the twentieth century emergence of psychoanalysis, which shows the difficulty at the heart of this effort toward self-knowledge. Whatever criticisms one would wish to make of the term unconscious, and there are many that are essential, the difficulty at the heart of the Socratic maxim is the barrier between conscious knowledge and the dynamic processes that build walls on the margins of the conscious mind.[1]

Mary Shelley's story is a dramatic example—one might even say a case study—of those processes of walling off those aspects of oneself that one does not wish to know.

Who is the Monster?[2]

Victor Frankenstein never considers this question of "Who is the Monster?" He is sure that the thing that he created is the monster, so he does not see his own disfigured image reflected in the eyes of his Monster. He is blind to his own monstrous deeds. The power of the question, then, is that it is the "Other" who has been negated, the one who has been cast aside, who poses it. The Monster speaking from the margins brings the question to us.

The *Frankenstein Prophecies* lingers on the margins to attend to this question and to listen to its unfolding in the Monster's untold tale. Working on the margins *The Frankenstein Prophecies* is a therapeutic engagement of the cultural-historically invented spectator mind personified in the figure of Victor Frankenstein.[3]

How to make a monster

Monsters come in many forms but the processes by which they are made have a psychological pattern. Whatever the guise in which they appear all of them are created on that steep descending slope of denial of responsibility for one's actions, which expresses itself in judgments of negation that demonize others.

Racism is an obvious example. Black is not white and it is the negation that turns one into an alien "Other." Religious bigotry is another example. Christian is not Jew and neither Jew nor Christian is Muslim. Slicing and dicing our way into more and more narrow comfort zones, the "Other" grows more numerous and ominous. Protestants are not Catholics, Sunnis are not Shiites, and Orthodox Jews are not reformed. We see the results of this splitting in wars that have their psychological ground in finding the monster in the "Other" who is not us.

The list seems endless and the sense of being "Other" has many forms, but the experience of being negated as "Other" is the same. If, for example, you are old in America you are "Other" in a culture that aspires to be forever young. Thinning gray hair, less than pearly white teeth, stooped posture and slow gait are not signs of a different and unique stage of life, not to say even perhaps signs of wisdom. On the contrary, they are marks of otherness that push one to the side. Watch TV commercials for Viagra or other male potency drugs and you get the point. Or watch those commercials designed for women that hawk vanishing creams and you begin to see those wrinkles that greet you in the morning reflection of the mirror not as signs of character but as paths of exile carved into the flesh. In place of these exiled impotent men and wrinkly women, the images of a virile, potent and erect male and a smooth skinned woman, who are often white, offer a story of youthful and privileged bliss.

Of course, the degrees of suffering in the many different ways of being "Othered" vary, and yet what is common to all of them is how difficult and often seemingly impossible it is for one who has been exiled as the "Other" to be recognized and to have a place, as this story about World War I dramatically illustrates:

On the first Christmas Eve of that war in December 1914 the soldiers of the German army and those of Great Britain ceased their hostilities and ventured forth from their trenches. Through Christmas carols sung on each side, and small gifts exchanged they were for a while not enemies. But when the sun rose the next morning and on orders from the high command on each side, the slaughter began again. Those who were brothers in the night became in the first rays of sunlight the "Other." Each became the enemy of the "Other," and the slaughter continued for four years.

One year after the horrors of World War I had ended, the Irish poet William Butler Yeats wrote these words: "And what rough beast, its hour come round at last, / Slouches towards Bethlehem to be born?"[4]

So, "Who is the Monster?"

What rough beasts linger on the horizon?

Examples abound!

Do we detect a rough beast in the too bright flash of light and the billowing mushroom cloud of radioactive particles that burst forth with the atomic age? Have our own powerful scientific and technological capacities for destruction become the coldblooded split off pieces of the collective Promethean mind?

Have our own creations become our monsters?

On the 75th anniversary of Pearl Harbor, which was the doorway to the atomic bombings of Hiroshima and Nagasaki, President Obama met with Shinzo Abe, the Prime Minister of Japan. The words of warning that President Obama spoke on that occasion recognize the lethal consequences of those processes that produce monsters:

We must resist the urge to demonize those who are different.

To hear these words is to go to the margins where we might meet the monster and perhaps even regard the monster as a radical teacher.

Margins, monsters and moonlight

In Question Two we witnessed the Monster's promised mate ripped to pieces by his maker Victor Frankenstein, and we understood that moment as one in the long line of Victor's sacrifice of the feminine in his work. We also read that act of violence as a prophetic anticipation of the dying of Nature as we know it.

At the end of Question Six we stood outside the window of Victor Frankenstein's laboratory alongside the Monster, sensing some of the hope that he felt for the first time in his brief but tortured loneliness. We were there with him too when that hope turned into despair as we watched by the light of the moon this final destructive act of Victor Frankenstein's dream. But in that moonlight we also caught a faint flicker of something else, a hint in the play of light and shadow from which arose this question: Do we see in that soft light, so different from the light of the solar mind of his maker, the beauty of the Monster?

To that question we add now these other questions:

Is it in moonlight that we also catch a glimpse of some new level of awareness about who is the Monster?

And, is it in moonlight and on the margins where we might find the seeds of a prophetic anticipation of a radical kind of ethics within Mary Shelley's novel?[5]

Let us remain in moonlight as we raise the question "Who is the Monster?" Let us seek an answer away from the solar light of the Promethean mind that created and abandoned the Monster to exile on the margins. Perhaps in moonlight and on the margins we might even find ourselves able to welcome Victor Frankenstein's Monster and celebrate his presence.

Dreaming in moonlight

Are we truly such stuff as dreams are made on?[6]

Are our lives rounded out in that little sleep that brings one back to oneself?

Are dreams expressions of wishes of who or what one might be?

Apart from any particular theories about the meaning of dreams, psychoanalysis begins with the dream as the path into the ignorance at the heart of our knowing, as the path that leads one into what has been walled off from the conscious mind.

Victor Frankenstein is born from Mary Shelley's dream, and his nightmarish dream immediately after his Monster awakens displays the dark side of her story.[7]

If we are to understand her story as a prophecy of a radical ethics, we have to make a place for the dream as an expression of moonlight wisdom. If we are to be with the Monster in moonlight, then we need to attend to the radical difference between moonlight and the light of Victor Frankenstein's solar mind.

In the bright light of the solar mind, that Promethean will that leaps toward the sun, one frames a question and then penetrates it. In the softer, darker light of the moon, one is framed by a question and is called to face it.

Dreaming and being dreamed

St Augustine, one of the early bright lights of Christianity, once stated that he thanked God he was not responsible for his dreams. It was and is an apt observation.[8]

We are not responsible for our dreams because when we are dreaming we are in fact being dreamed. It is only when one wakes up that he or she says, "I had a dream," when in fact the dream has had the dreamer.

Augustine's observation is, therefore, incomplete because we are responsible for what we make of our dreams. Apart from whatever a dream may mean, each dream is a question that addresses one with possibilities. In the dream world, one is portrayed in ways that have been un-imagined. We might even say that in this context each dream is a vocation and one is called to face the question and consider its possibilities.

Victor Frankenstein, however, does not face the possibility that in the dream's wisdom the figure of his dead mother shows the dark side of his desire to be a new creator god who would exile death from life through the powers of science and technology. The question posed by her image of whether he should create life even if he has the power to do so does not enter his mind. Instead he runs away and begins his continuous denial of responsibility for his actions.

Victor Frankenstein sides with Augustine's incomplete observation. In the dream where Victor Frankenstein happily embraces his beloved Elizabeth Lavenza, he discovers in horror that he is embracing the rotting corpse of his dead mother. In that dream image Frankenstein's Promethean mind is faced with a question about the ethics of his work.

Of course, his refusal to consider his nightmarish dream is what makes Mary Shelley's story the tragedy that has endured. Indeed, its tragedy is what makes her story the pivotal and prophetic work it is, and it creates a place for *The Frankenstein Prophecies* to go to the margins to be with the Monster in moonlight and attend to the Monster's untold tale in her story. On the margins and in moonlight, *The Frankenstein Prophecies* takes up Victor Frankenstein's dream as a possibility that brings to the fore the issue of the willed ignorance at the core of our ways of knowing. Doing so, *The Frankenstein Prophecies* focuses on the question of Mary Shelley's story as a prophecy of a radical ethics.

Toward a radical ethics

A radical ethics is an ethics for the margins. It is a key issue of this book and the turning point where *The Frankenstein Prophecies* looks at Victor Frankenstein's work and dream through a psychological lens.

This lens offers another perspective on the pivotal character of Mary Shelley's story. Imagining Victor Frankenstein as a modern Prometheus, she frames her story in those cultural and historical conditions that made her work possible and perhaps even necessary. In *The Frankenstein Prophecies* a psychological reading of her story shows that these conditions, while having been forgotten, still linger on the margins of mind as a collective amnesia. As such, her story lives on in prophetic implications that display the lethal and destructive consequences of Victor Frankenstein's denial of the responsibilities he owed to the Monster he made. These prophetic consequences have haunted the collective mind in the guise of the many seemingly monstrous crises we face today brought on by the uncritical and unexamined use and abuse of our technological god like powers.

Mary Shelley's story personifies and dramatizes the psychological dynamics at work in making a monster. The characters of Victor Frankenstein and his Monster are images that stir the depths of the human heart and can shake up for a moment the fixed beliefs in whatever facts and ideas we might have about monsters. Moreover, the endurance of her story seems to indicate our vague familiarity with what has been made into the "other," and our fascination with the monstrous, with what, having been walled off from the rational mind, and having been exiled to the margins, can be seen but at a safe distance.

But even at a safe distance does our sense of difference from the "monstrous other" become, perhaps at least for a moment, disturbed?

On the margins are we questioned anew and measured by something other than ourselves, by a measure which the Promethean mind of Victor Frankenstein erased?

If so, is that moment an opening toward a radical ethics and its question, "Who is the Monster?"

Perhaps!

I say perhaps because we know that that moment can also be a moment when we increase the distance between the "monstrous other" and ourselves. Indeed, Victor Frankenstein is the emblem of that reaction. The Monster that he has made and exiled is cursed as devil and demon. It is a moment when the fatal attraction we seem to have with all that is labeled as evil comes too close and cuts to the bone.

If we are to keep the possibility of a radical ethics that is latent in Mary Shelley's story alive, we need to explore the psychological roots of denial as a process of walling off those aspects of oneself that one does not wish to know.

Building psychological walls

Denying responsibility for his actions, Victor Frankenstein takes his first step away from any ethical concerns about his work. Denial is, as it were, the first brick that Victor Frankenstein uses in walling himself off from what he has created.

But that denial that he displays by running away and by fainting at the initial sight of his creation is not sufficient. The Monster that he sees is now not only alive in the world, he is also alive in his dreams, as testified by the nightmare he has of his dead mother. Living in him as his ongoing suffering, as his anxiety and at time his despair, the Monster that Victor Frankenstein has walled off requires a wall within himself. The bricks and mortar of that wall are made when Victor Frankenstein splits off the Monster from how he wishes to see himself. But divided within himself, Victor Frankenstein ultimately is torn apart by what he has denied, and in this act of splitting, it is Victor Frankenstein who pays the price, as it were, for building his wall. The Monster has become his twin, the other side of himself as real and as alive as he is. In the too bright light of his solar mind, the dark shadow of himself cast by that light follows him wherever he goes.[9]

But even this brick is not enough. The wall is not high enough or strong enough to keep the Monster at bay. A third brick needs to be put in place and Victor Frankenstein does so when he presents himself to Captain Walton as the innocent victim of the Monster he made. Even as he is dying, he seeks to remain in his own eyes and to Walton the benefactor who wanted only to remove the curse of death from humanity. He insists even to the end that all the destruction and death are the fault of the Monster. He projects onto the Monster the reasons for the failure of his dream.

Mary Shelley's story is a psychological exegesis that dramatically portrays how the psychological processes of denial, splitting and projection create monsters that are exiled to the margins of mind. These psychological processes of wall building are what stand in the way of a radical ethics. If one is to take up the possibility of a prophecy of a radical ethics in her work, a place has to be made for understanding these psychological dynamics, which are personified in the relation between Victor Frankenstein and his Monster. These dynamics are at work in the multiple crises we face today that are the prophetic amplifications of Mary Shelley's story. But these dynamics often have little if any place in the philosophical, scientific, political and economic approaches to these crises.[10]

Going to the margins to lend an ear to the Monster's untold tale, *The Franken-stein Prophecies* attends to these dynamics. This approach is a necessary complement to other approaches; it is also what makes this work a challenge. It is, moreover, a challenge not only to the reader but also to myself as the writer as the question— "Who is the Monster?"—has been continuously drawing me closer and closer to the edge, to the margins where the Monster waits to question me even as I have been posing questions. Indeed, I sense that in order to do this marginal work, one has to become what one wishes to know.[11]

On the individual level, this is a difficult task. That difficulty is magnified almost beyond comparison when such marginal work is also to be done on the collective level of our shared cultural dreams. The Monster who has been exiled to the margins is also living on in these collective dreams in the guises of those crises we have explored in this book.

Marginal questions

The Frankenstein Prophecies emphasizes not only the necessity of the question. It also focuses on questions that arise on the margins of mind and such questions differ in a fundamental way from other kinds of questions. There are, for example, questions that arise from the narrative flow of the work. These questions are like a flashing yellow light, a signal to move forward but with caution. A second kind of question is more like a traffic sign that indicates that one is to slow down. Slowing down creates a little space to pause for a brief moment to sense what might pass by too quickly as the story moves forward. In this space there is time to attend to possibilities and implications that arise while the story is progressing. Indeed, these questions seem to appear as if from some side road, and they invite another view of what has seemed to be a settled matter about where one is going.

Marginal questions are radically different. Neither a flashing yellow light nor a speed warning sign, marginal questions are like a sinkhole that has unexpectedly opened up in the road. As such they do more than slow us down. Rising up from below and seeping through the fissures on the road taken by the story, these questions stop us in our tracks. Challenging the conviction that we are even the ones who ask the questions, these questions turn us upside down and inside out. They question us.

In this regard, these questions are like dreams, which invert the relation between the dreamer and the dream. It is only when we wake up and restore the hegemony of the waking mind that we say we had a dream, when in fact we are dreamed by the dream. These sinkhole questions, then, add the dimension of depth to margins. As such, they warn us that to go to the margins is to fall into what is not only unexpected but also still unknown. In this regard, marginal questions are like medieval maps, which show dragons at the margins of the known world.

The dragons on the margins of maps of the medieval world are our monsters on the margins of the ways we have technologically mapped our world. Then and now the challenge is to face them. To stay with the analogy to traffic signs, the state of disrepair in our roads, which is such a prevalent question today for our state and federal governments, might address us from the margins as more than an economic issue to be solved with more money. This sinkhole question might reveal the fissures in the collective dream of the spectator mind, which, in measuring and mapping the world from a distance, frames everything as a technical problem. Such kinds of questions, then, might take us down roads less traveled.

"Who is the Monster?" is a sinkhole question. It is the marginal question posed by the untold tale in Mary Shelley's story. It is the Monster's question that is posed to us, the question that radically questions our denial of his existence, the question that questions our placing what is monstrous on the "Other" and banishing that monstrous other to the margins. The ability to be questioned in this way is the ground of a radical ethics that faces us with what has been and still is unsaid in all that has been said about the Monster.

There is that brief moment when Victor Frankenstein has a doubt about whether he should attempt to create life. In that doubt there is the seed of an ethical question. Just because he has the power to create life, should he do so? But the temptation to become a new god tramples the doubt under his feet as he rushes head long into his work.

In 1976 Joseph Weizenbaum published *Computer Power and Human Reason: From Judgment to Calculation*. In his book he asked his version of Victor Frankenstein's question: If we have the means to do something does that mean we should do it?

An early pioneer in the field of artificial intelligence he had the credentials to make a strong case that however powerful computers might become they would lack the human capacities of compassion and wisdom.

As the capacity of computer technology has exponentially increased since that date, does his question now seem naïve?

Indeed, has it all but disappeared?

In 2005 Ray Kurzweil published *The Singularity is Near: When Humans Transcend Biology*. As we saw in Question Five, his book is an emphatic yes to both questions. 1976 to 2005!

In less than thirty years from Weizenbaum's hesitation and questioning attitude to Kurzweil's unquestioning, confident and optimistic embrace of the possibilities offered by the accelerating powers of our technological knowledge, our human capacities for compassion and wisdom are becoming more and more challenged. In that gap of less than thirty years, judgment as an essential aspect of human reason has gradually but continuously given way to a fascination with calculation and its promise of greater speed. Just recall all the ads that pop up on our computer screens for making our computers faster. Moreover, in that same gap human intelligence has been progressively reframed as information, as bits of data.

Compassion is a quality that allows us to understand the other's suffering and to be with that other in his or her suffering as a companion. As such it is a slow process, which not only takes time but also presence. It is the emotional dimension of human intelligence as well as a dimension in many species of animals. It is the capacity that gives human and animal intelligence its relational and situational qualities.

Wisdom too takes time as it incubates knowledge, and in relation to information it is as the tortoise to the hare. Wisdom cannot be forced or rushed. It is a quality that is displayed in the wise philosopher, the patient poet and the cautious science researcher questioning and re-questioning his or her results. When human intelligence becomes calculative thinking with its emphasis on the quantity of information gathered and the speed in which it can be transmitted, wisdom is imperiled. When compassion and wisdom are swamped in speed, Weizenbaum's question is sacrificed and our question "Who is the Monster?" seems less and less possible.

Victor Frankenstein is an avatar of one who lacks compassion and wisdom and his story is a cautionary tale of how their absence creates a Monster. It is a tale that makes us wonder: "Where is the wisdom we have lost in knowledge, the knowledge we have lost in information?"[12]

An inconvenient truth

The 2006 the documentary film, *An Inconvenient Truth*, featured Al Gore's attempts to raise public awareness about the crisis of global warming, which he has followed up with *An Inconvenient Sequel: Truth to Power*, which premiered in 2017. In between the two films Leonardo Di Caprio's 2016 documentary, *Before The Flood*, has continued this effort.

The global climate crisis is one of the issues that we explored as a prophecy in Mary Shelley's story. In Question Two we examined how the dying of nature as we know it has its roots in those cultural-historical conditions that made nature into a spectacle separated from the disembodied spectator mind. Apart from nature and no longer a part of it, the spectator mind subjected the animate, living quality of nature to its calculations.

In the ten-year period between Gore's first film and Di Caprio's documentary, the living spirit of nature, as Gore's second film emphasizes, has been increasingly imperiled as the dangers of global warming have accelerated and continue to do so. But in that same ten year period public awareness of the dangers has grown. As strange as it might seem, this increase in danger and public awareness might very well herald a shift toward the Monster on the margins. It might be the beginning of a shift toward that radical ethics, which might allow us to hear the question "Who is the Monster?" because the climate crisis as a global crisis is simultaneously local:

Every person on the planet and all the animals and all living things breathe air, so do not ask for whom the air is polluted, it is polluted for you.

Every person on the planet and all the animals and all living things need water, so do not ask for whom the water is fouled, it is fouled for you.

Every person on the planet and all the animals and all living things need the earth, so do not ask for whom the earth is being flooded or subjected to drought, it is being flooded and desiccated for you.

And every person on the planet and all the animals and all living things need the fire of the sun, so do not ask for whom that fire is melting the polar regions of the world, the ice caps are melting for you.

As the seventeenth century English poet John Donne said about the bell that tolls for death, "Do not ask for whom the bell tolls, it tolls for thee," the global climate crisis that is also local is, moreover, elemental.[13]

Do not ask therefore about who is imperiled by the threats to air, water, earth and the fire of the sun, for these elements link us all together regardless of our personal, cultural and geographical differences. The bell that is tolling the dying of Nature as we know it is tolling for all of us and perhaps for all the animals and all living things.

The Monster's questions from the margins are elemental questions. They are basic, fundamental and radical.

They are radical because they go to the root of who we are, reminding all of us that we are a part of nature and cannot, without peril to ourselves and all living things, act as if we are apart from nature.

They are fundamental because at bottom the Monster's questions humble the spectator mind.

And they are basic because such marginal questions not only restore the broken connection of Nature and Mind; they also awaken Mind to its origins from within Nature.

To be responsive to the prophetic possibilities in Mary Shelley's tale is marginal work, and that work requires a shift toward that radical ethics that faces each of us with an inconvenient truth. That truth is the Monster's truth, the truth that lies in his question about who is the monster.

A closing word

But, as we have seen, marginal work is a difficult challenge because it requires that we take responsibility for what we have individually and collectively denied, split off from ourselves, projected onto the "Other" and exiled that "Other" to the margins. It requires that we own what we have individually and collectively denied. It requires that we "become" the Monster.

But what does that mean?

Does it mean that we identify with what is monstrous?

Does it mean that we literally become monstrous?

Does it mean that behave monstrously?

No!

The Monster on the margins is not who or what we are. On the contrary, the Monster is an emotionally real presence that mirrors us like a character on stage mirrors us. Like the dramatic presence of such characters is neither a matter of fact nor an idea of mind, but is nevertheless so real that it can change and transform us, the literary figure of the Monster born of Mary Shelley's dream can change who and how we are in relation to the crises spawned by Victor Frankenstein's dream to act as if we have godlike powers.

Having escaped the dichotomy of what is outside in the world and inside our minds, the Monster lives on in that subtle powerful space of the cultural imagination. In the guise of climate crisis, or in those other guises we have explored as prophetic possibilities in Mary Shelley's work, he challenges us to regard these crises in another way, from his point of view and thus re-imagine other possibilities within them.

There is evidence that the Monster on the margins with his disturbing question is making his way into the cultural imagination. In a recent film, *A Monster Calls*,[14] a young boy fears the impending loss of his dying mother, and when she does die he is unable to grieve. But he is finally brought deeply into his grief by the insistent power of a huge tree that stands in his garden. Repeatedly in the film that tree is framed through the boy's bedroom window as he prepares to sleep. These images have a brooding, haunting quality to them as if the tree knows what the young boy fears. In the final scenes of the film the tree awakens the boy to his fears as he falls into his sorrow.

The parallels of this film with the story of Victor Frankenstein seem obvious. As we have seen throughout this work, it is the death of his mother that drives Victor Frankenstein into his project to erase death from life, and it is his refusal to grieve her loss that gives his story the shape of tragedy. Death and the denial of grief over loss create his Monster. In addition, the tree in the young boy's garden is a living tree, a tree that is alive in his dreams and his imagination. It is not the blasted tree trunk destroyed by lightning in Victor's story. In the film it is the animate spirit of nature that redeems the young boy. In Victor's story it is the destructive power of nature, the force that brings death, that dominates his life.

And yet, still we must acknowledge that marginal monster work is a challenge, which seems so often to be too much. But as challenging as this work might be, it seems necessary. If we do not work on the margins, we not only support without awareness the cultural dreams in which we are ensnared, we also abet the on going continuation of those dreams.

Does Mary Shelley's story place that necessity before us?

Might it even be the case that this marginal monster work is now necessary for our very survival?

Is the Monster on the margins, with his untold tale at the heart of which is the question "Who is the Monster?" the best hope—the last?—for nature, for earth, and for ourselves?

The possibility of a radical ethics is a seed of hope, one of the seeds of hope to be harvested from Mary Shelley's prophetic story. In Question Eight we shall harvest a few more of those seeds.

Notes

1 The walls we build outside ourselves are also walls that are within us. What one represses inside becomes what one oppresses outside and vice versa. Repression and oppression are two sides of one coin. When one takes psychological dynamics seriously, then one has to frame Trump's wall in a way that highlights its dangers. The irony here is that while he wants to build such a wall to keep the "other" at bay, the silenced voices of the "others"—women, blacks, the poor and young people who have had enough of the NRA's politics—are shouting on the margins of the collective mind. For a rigorous defense of the reality of unconscious dynamics, which is also insightfully critical of its philosophical foundations, see Paul Ricoeur (1970).

2 The ability to be questioned in this way is the ground of a radical ethics that faces us with what has been and still is unsaid in all that has been said about the Monster. If we are deaf to this question, then, as Jung has noted, what we do not face in ourselves we do meet as our fate in the world. The eight Questions explored in *The Frankenstein Prophecies* are invitations to attend to the Monster in the guises of the monstrous problems we face today, and, perhaps, in doing so a chance to transform fate that seems fixed into opportunities to be re-imagined.

3 Literature is embodied psychology, dramatically enacted and personified. As such, *The Frankenstein Prophecies* brings in the psychological dimension of eight crises we face today without using psychological jargon. This approach is what makes this book unique for the psychological aspect is pretty much absent in the scientific, economic, technological and political approaches to the crises spawned by our unchecked use of our god like powers. From a psychological point of view that makes a place for unconscious dynamics, the crises we face are not just a matter of incomplete scientific data, or the economic costs involved in weaning our civilization from its fossil fuel addiction, or the lack of technological abilities, or the absence of a political will to make changes. All of these factors matter, but if we stay only at these levels of the crises and ignore the psychological factor of unconscious dynamics at play in all these debates, we are wasting our time as we approach a turning point of inevitable disaster.

In this context, *The Frankenstein Prophecies* is a reply to Per Espen Stoknes's book *What We Think About When We Try Not To Think About Global Warming* (2015). What we do think about is anything but climate crises as the monster we have made.

While Stoknes's book is an excellent and extensive discussion of the many and various strategies of climate crisis denial, there is scant discussion of the key role of unconscious dynamics in creating these strategies. In this regard, his book could serve as a wakeup call to recognize that we have our heads in the clouds regarding the unconscious motives at work in climate crisis. The front cover of the book is a clever image of this point. Coffee in hand, well suited and tied, the man with his head in the clouds—could it be a mushroom cloud?—is an emblem of all of us who have to wake up and take on the most dangerous task we face today: the danger of thinking from the depths, on the margins and alongside the monsters we have made.

4 Yeats (1919/1956). The poem from which this quote is taken is "The Second Coming." Written in the aftermath of World War I and the coming Irish War for Independence, the use of Christian imagery in the context of the devastation of these wars situates the second coming as a beast that is now slouching toward Bethlehem. In the context of *The Frankenstein Prophecies* that beast is the monstrous shadow of death that Victor Frankenstein would erase from the human condition.

5 Jung's *Answer to Job* (1958/1973) is one of his most radical and important books because it does challenge the Christian ethic that splits Jesus from the Devil, an ethics that rests on St Augustine's splitting good from evil and regarding evil as the absence of the good (*privatio boni*). In his book Jung describes the dark side of Yaweh and explores the ways in which Job carries the ethical dimension of Yaweh. For Jung this seminal work regards evil as a source in its own right.

6 Shakespeare (1623/2000). The words are spoken by Prospero in Act IV, Scene 1 of *The Tempest*. Often the line is misread as "we are such stuff as dreams are made *of*," which would suggest that for Prospero the spirits, like the world of dreams, and the play itself, is an illusion. But read as "we are such stuff as dreams are made *on*," the line suggests rather differently that the fabric of our lives is made by dreams, that our lives are dreamlike and as such do matter. *The Frankenstein Prophecies* argues for the validity, value and wisdom of the dream, which, as we saw, the spectator mind of Victor Frankenstein ignores with fatal consequences.

7 Mary Shelley's story anticipates Freud's explorations of the dream as the royal road to the unconscious mind. From the perspective of psychoanalysis, then, one could interpret Victor's dream as an Oedipal wound when he never fully grieved the death of his mother. Along this same line one could then also interpret Victor's action of destroying the mate he promised to make for his Monster as an act of revenge against the mother who had abandoned him in her dying. Indeed, the eclipse of the feminine in Victor's work can be regarded as rooted in this complex.

But, while I acknowledge this way of reading Shelley's story, I follow a different path in *The Frankenstein Prophecies*. A psychoanalytic reading stays on the symbolic level where the Monster is Victor's burden. In this regard we miss how in attending to the untold tale of the Monster, he exists, like fictional characters in film and theater do, as a real presence that lingers and haunts the collective mind.

The difference is more than a mere preference. Indeed, the difference concerns how we regard the issue of evil. Is it only a psychological issue rooted in unconscious desires? Is it real in itself, a force of nature, which perhaps finds its way into the human world through unconscious dynamics?

This latter view is more in line with the work of Carl Jung. Within the context of his psychology, Question Seven brings in a psychological perspective that makes a place for the lingering and haunting presence of the Monster. The Monster created then denied and abandoned by his creator comes to us through Victor's unconscious, but he is not simply about Victor's unconscious. What Victor created, denied and abandoned he meets as his fate. The prophetic character of Mary Shelley's story is that as we continue Victor's dream we continue to meet the Monster as our collective fate in the symptomatic disguises we explore in this book.

For a very recent and excellent Jungian account of the question of evil, see Lionel Corbett's *Understanding Evil: A Psychotherapist's Guide* (2018).

8 Augustine as quoted in Neumann (1973, p. 74). See Romanyshyn (2007, Chapter 13) for a thorough discussion of how Augustine's thanks to God is a one sided Christian ethic.

9 In an earlier draft of this book some scenes were performed like this one with Victor Frankenstein standing on stage, haunted, anxious, looking around. At first he is in weak light, but then the light becomes brighter and as it does the looming shadow cast by himself, grows larger and more ominous. He screams and the light goes out.

10 If this book is imagined as a theater piece then another way to make a scene would be to imagine Socrates on the couch describing to Freud his punishment for questioning the gods. The scene would dramatically portray how difficult this work toward a radical ethics can be: Socrates is murdered by the state, and Freud's patients become neurotic, which amounts to psychological murder. But we do not have to imagine it as theater for such a drama is being enacted collectively with Donald Trump's fantasy of building a border wall between the USA and Mexico. It is a drama staged in the political arena and presented to his audience of supporters who project their fears onto the "Other."

11 In *The Wounded Researcher* (2007), I described how, in making a place for unconscious dynamics in the research process, the researcher is claimed by the work, drawn into it, through his or her complex, unconscious ties with the work. I also described and illustrated with numerous examples from my students that the task of a truly ethical epistemology requires that the researcher make his or her unconscious dynamics as conscious as possible. Doing so through a series of active imagination exercises described in the book, the researcher is continuously being faced with questions like "who is doing the work, and for whom is the work being done?" Such ongoing reflections frame the issue that Victor Frankenstein too quickly dismisses: Should the work be done? He does not know who he is, nor does he pause long enough to consider the consequences that come to him only in his nightmare dream of his dead mother.

The Wounded Researcher argues that for an ethical epistemology to be possible one has to become what one wishes to know. And this is the difficult challenge because it does not mean one identifies with the work. This is what Victor Frankenstein does. He becomes the god who imagines that he will and can create life. In place of this dangerous identification, one has to imagine oneself in terms of the possibilities opened up by the work, like one might imagine what it is like to live as if one were a character seen in a play. One has to keep the imagination fertile and be vigilant for those moments when it weakens and one slips into an unconscious identification. As the examples in the book show, such signs of identification often come through one's symptoms and in one's dreams.

The Frankenstein Prophecies is an example of this last point. While working on the book I discovered I had to have cataract surgery. In addition, I needed two stitches in my left heel to heal a deep cut and I had tendonitis in my right knee making it difficult to walk. Indeed with eye patch over left eye and walking awkwardly my wife said I had become like the Monster. I was embodying his tale.

12 Eliot (1934, p. 81). Regarding my claim that Victor Frankenstein lacks compassion and wisdom the recent Netflix series *The Frankenstein Chronicles* (2015) dramatically illustrates this claim.

13 See Question Six, note seven.

14 *A Monster Calls* (2016). Written by Patrick Ness and directed by J. A. Bayna.

Question Eight

OTHER SEEDS OF HOPE IN MARY SHELLEY'S STORY

Is Mary Shelley's story a prophecy of new beginnings?

The last visit

As Victor Frankenstein is dying, his last words to Captain Robert Walton emphasize once again his innocence regarding the monstrous outcomes of his work: "During these last days I have been occupied in examining my past conduct; nor do I find it blameable" (Shelley, 1818).

Confessing that his work was done "In a fit of enthusiastic madness," he claims that his obligation toward his creature "to assure, as far as was in my power, his happiness and well-being," was overtaken by a greater claim he had "toward my fellow creatures ... because they included a greater proportion of happiness or misery."

It is a convincing argument, and yet its ethics seems to be an expression of his utilitarian values that he adopted at the outset of his work, and its motive a rationalization of his actions.

But to cite these passages is not to judge a dying man's words, but to note that his words are the context he offers to Walton regarding that fateful moment when he destroyed the mate he had promised to make to assuage the "Monster's" loneliness. Because his duties to his fellow creatures outweighed those toward the Monster he made, he says, "I refused, and I did right in refusing, to create a companion for the first creature."

At this point, Walton notes that Victor Frankenstein's voice "became fainter as he spoke; and at length, exhausted by his effort, he sunk into silence" (Shelley, 1818). But as Walton continues his bedside vigil, Victor opens his eyes once more and tries to speak. He is, however, too weak to do so, and taking hold of Walton's hand, Victor takes his final breath. Walton's comment on this moment attests to his place as a witness of Victor's claim of innocence. He says that as Victor died "the irradiation of a gentle smile passed away from his lips" (Shelley, 1818).

Victor Frankenstein appears to have died a peaceful man.

But what about his Monster?

Is he at peace?

And what about us who are living in the prophetic wake of Victor's work?

Are we at peace?

As Walton writes of the sorrow that he feels over "the untimely extinction of this glorious spirit," the Monster enters. He has come to seek Victor's acknowledgment and perhaps some small sign of redemption. But his maker is dead. His creator god, who, even to the very end, remains blind to his responsibilities for the tragedies that followed his "madness," cannot pardon him. The Monster, however, admitting his responsibilities for the destructive acts he committed, is not at peace. Tortured by guilt for what he has done, he accepts his suffering and yet still seeks at least to tell his side of the story. Walton then becomes a witness to this untold tale, which, however, he refuses to condone. To the very end Walton is Victor Frankenstein's advocate and the one through whom that side of the story has endured, while the Monster has remained a monster whose side of the story has been largely silenced and marginalized.

Chastised by Walton for what seems to him a "superfluous" act of repentance by the Monster for his deeds, the Monster begins a long series of remarks, which express the suffering visited upon him by the actions of his maker. These remarks elaborate the way in which he has already educated himself regarding the relation between a creator and his creation by reading John Milton's *Paradise Lost*. Coming to understand himself as the new Adam, we can imagine that the words that the biblical Adam poses to God in Milton's epic poem would weigh heavily on the Monster's own heart.

> Did I request thee, Maker, from my clay
> To mould me man? Did I solicit thee
> From darkness to promote me?[1]
> *(Shelley, 1818)*

He did not and to Walton he wants to say not only that his maker failed him in refusing to fulfill his obligations to him, but also that, as a consequence of his maker's abandoning him, he has suffered as much and perhaps even more than has Victor Frankenstein. "My heart was fashioned to be susceptible of love and sympathy," he says to Walton, adding, "and when wrenched by misery to vice and hatred, it did not endure the violence of the change without torture, such as you cannot even imagine." Recalling his murder of Victor's companion and friend Henry Clerval, he asks Walton, "Think ye that the groans of Clerval were music to my ears?" (Shelley, 1818).

It is not a surprise that Walton regards the Monster's speech with suspicion, believing he is seeking only to absolve himself by shifting all the blame onto his creator. After all that is the way the story has been told and has endured, portraying Victor Frankenstein as worthy of praise for his dream and his work and the Monster as the spoiler. We should not be surprised, then, that Walton as Victor's advocate remains deaf to the Monster's words and continues those very same processes that demonized him from the beginning and which created him as the Monster.

But then that small seed of hope that lies on the margins of Mary Shelley's story, that tiny seed that has fallen by the wayside of the collective spectator mind, the possibility of transformation that lies in the Monster's tale, is lost. To prevent that loss we have to listen to these words of the Monster that he addresses to Walton shortly before he quits the ship and goes into the Arctic night where he intends to immolate himself:

> You, who call Frankenstein your friend, seem to have a knowledge of my crimes and his misfortunes. But, in the detail which he gave you of them, he could not sum up the hours and months of misery which I endured, wasting in impotent passions.
>
> *(Shelley, 1818)*

The devil, it is said, is in the details. The details have been left out of Victor Frankenstein's telling of the story. Those details are in the "Monster's" tale.

Love as a seed of hope: July 17, 2016

St Peter's Church, Bournemouth, England! Late afternoon on a warm summer's day! It is to this place that I have followed the track of the Monster, to a church-yard cemetery, that kind of place, which was for Victor the unhallowed soil from which he dug up the body parts needed to make his creature.

But this cemetery ground is sacred and what are buried here are not, as Victor Frankenstein claimed, bodies merely deprived of life. Bodies of persons buried with rituals of remembrance lay here, not impersonal, anonymous corpses. Indeed, as I wander among the gravestones, stories of who they were are etched in stone, and as I stop and linger for a moment with the dead I am stitched into a history, woven into the large pattern of humanity in the journey from cradle to grave. And the dead when remembered live again for a moment.

On a small knoll above the churchyard I find the grave I have come to see. The tombstone confirms that I am standing before the grave of Mary Shelley, who was interred here in 1851.

But this grave tells me something more. This lapidary story tells me not only that she is in her grave alongside her father, William Godwin, and her mother, Mary Wollstonecraft, but also in the company of her husband Percy Bysshe Shelley's heart.[2]

Her husband's heart!

This detail stands out. Standing by the side of this grave, her story becomes a mystery. Here the story of Frankenstein continues and even takes on legendary proportions. It is a detail that transforms the story into a myth, which has given *Frankenstein; Or The Modern Prometheus* its extraordinary vitality. The power of the myth, the endurance of the story spins a spell around this gravesite that webs me in reverie.

Lingering at this gravesite where so few people now visit, I begin to find my place with those who are buried here, with Mary Shelley and her parents and especially with the heart of her husband.

We celebrate the heart as a symbol of love and devotion and I remember that the Monster, whose mate was destroyed before his eyes, and whose maker was unable to love what he created, was condemned to the margins to be alone forever in his isolation and misery.

Forced to live without love did he become monstrous?

In Question Three I suggested that Mary Shelley's story is a love story, or to be more accurate a narrative about the complexities of love when love is corrupted by power. But buried beneath this distortion of love by power, there is that seed of hope about the redemptive power of love. It is a seed of hope to be nourished by attending to the relation between the Monster and his potential mate, a relation that is so different from that between Victor and Elizabeth Lavenza. It is a seed that displays itself at the site of the grave, a seed that contains the intimate bond between love and death.

So, as I linger at Mary Shelley's grave, I wonder about the Monster. Although Mary Shelley finished writing her story in 1817, her story and its dream are not done. Does the Monster's story continue here? Is this gravesite the ground where he too must have a place, where he can be mourned and as such become part of the human community? Mourned and remembered does he finally receive a small measure of love?

We bury the dead with rituals of remembrance that promise to keep those who have died in our hearts. Remembering the dead, we bear witness to love as the force that does survive death, a power that is stronger than will. Poets are often bearers of this wisdom.

> Ah, love, let us be true
> To one another! for the world, which seems
> To lie before us like a land of dreams,
> So various, so beautiful, so new,
> Hath really neither joy, nor love, nor light,
> Nor certitude, nor peace, nor help for pain;
> And we are here as on a darkling plain
> Swept with confused alarms of struggle and flight,
> Where ignorant armies clash by night.
>
> *(Arnold, 1867/2012)*

These lines are the last stanza of Matthew Arnold's poem "Dover Beach." They are not heroic in their acknowledgment of life's sorrows in a newly industrialized world that has lost a sense of faith. But they are a melancholic testimony to the hope that love is the truth that allows one to bear, even in the face of a world where love itself seems to be only a dream, those sorrows. Moreover, written in 1851 just after his marriage to Frances Lucy Wightman, we might read these lines as an affirmation of love in its first bloom as what endures in its fading even into death.

What spoils this power of love for Victor Frankenstein is the great spoiler death.

In the face of death, Victor Frankenstein abandons love and allies himself with the power of his Promethean will to banish death from life. The genius of Mary Shelley's story is that she knows the tragic consequences of this dream to will death away.

Victor Frankenstein is a flawed god, who portrays for us a love story corrupted by the will to power. He portrays an inhuman love built upon a shaky ground that excludes not just the dark shadow of death, but also the shadows of betrayal, envy and jealousy among others.[3]

But in Bournemouth where Mary Shelley's story continues, love is a seed of hope. At the site of the grave love overcomes the will to power. At the site of Mary Shelley's grave, the rituals of burying our dead display themselves as moments where hope springs up, perhaps only for a moment, and stills, perhaps for a moment, our flight from death.

A mind for no seasons

When Victor Frankenstein begins to conceive of the possibility that he could create life, he wonders if he should take on that power and transgress the boundary between God and man. But he pauses only for a brief moment at this threshold, dismissing the moral and ethical dimensions of his work. He is, after all, a modern Prometheus, and, like his mythic namesake, he believes that crossing the boundary between the divine and human order is in the service of mankind.[4] Convinced of the rightness of his work, the issue that confronts him is not if he should continue but how he should do so. His concerns are practical ones:

> When I found so astonishing a power placed in my hands, I hesitated a long time concerning the manner in which I should employ it. Although I possessed the capacity of bestowing animation, yet to prepare a frame for the reception of it, with all its intricacies of fibers, muscles, and veins, still remained a work of inconceivable difficulty and labour.

Rejecting the idea that it would be easier to create a simpler being, he remains fully confident in his creative powers "to give life to an animal as complex and wonderful as man." So he forges ahead and begins the pivotal work that marks Mary Shelley's story as a dramatic threshold moment in the history of the spectator mind.

"As the minuteness of the parts formed a great hindrance to my speed, I resolved ... to make the being of a gigantic stature, that is to say, about eight feet in height, and proportionably large" (Shelley, 1818).

As a new God armed with the powers of science and technology to create life, Victor Frankenstein adopts a utilitarian attitude regarding his work. The values that inform his work are how quickly it can be done and the size of the being that will best serve that purpose. There is a kind of soulless quality in his attitude, a deadness that seems empty of any human qualities that are nourished by moral and ethical concerns.[5] It is not surprising, then, that the being he is creating will mirror this inhuman quality. Indeed, when Victor first sees what he has done he is shocked by the monstrous quality of its gigantic appearance.

There is a key moment in Mary Shelley's story when Victor Frankenstein becomes aware of the price he paid for the utilitarian attitude that drove his work. As he is dying, he offers this advice to Captain Walton: "The forms of the beloved dead flit before me, and I hasten to their arms. Farewell, Walton! Seek happiness in tranquility, and avoid ambition, even it be only the apparently innocent one of distinguishing yourself in science and discoveries" (Shelley, 1818).

There is a glimmer of insight in his words about what he sacrificed in pursuit of his dream to create life. But he quickly retracts this advice. Even in this hour of his death, which he now welcomes as a release, saying of this final hour, " it is the only happy one which I have enjoyed for several years," he adds, "Yet why do I say this? I have been blasted in these hopes, yet another may succeed" (Shelley, 1818).[6]

There are several other occasions in Mary Shelley's story, which depict Victor Frankenstein's ambivalence about the price he paid for his dream. As we saw in Question One, Victor Frankenstein does acknowledge that price when he says to Captain Walton, "I pursued nature to her hiding places and seemed to have lost all soul or sensation but for this one pursuit" (Shelley, 1818). As ironic as it is that he who would create life confesses to have lost his soul, he does seem to regret that loss:

> The summer months passed while I was thus engaged, heart and soul, in one pursuit. It was a most beautiful season; never did the fields bestow a more plentiful harvest, or the vines yield a more luxurious vintage: but my eyes were insensible to the charms of nature.[7]
>
> *(Shelley, 1818)*

These words contrast sharply with the utilitarian values of Victor's spectator mind. They reveal a mind sensitive to the seasons of nature and as he continues to describe this experience to Walton, a tone of self-criticism creeps into his words:

> If the study to which you apply yourself has a tendency to weaken your affections, and to destroy your taste for those simple pleasures in which no alloy can possibly mix, then that study is certainly unlawful, that is to say, not befitting the human mind.
>
> *(Shelley, 1818)*

There is more than a hint of confession in these words. They betray to Walton a warning that, in becoming insensible to the charms of nature, he was, so to speak, out of his mind.

Victor Frankenstein is a prototype of the mind for no seasons, whose dream of being a new creator god lives on today as a prophetic warning to us. His story is a cautionary tale to slow down the seemingly insane pace of our technological powers to create life and dominate nature. The irony here is that he, who would conquer death, realizes at the moment of his own dying that to override the laws of nature is unlawful.

That ironic twist in Mary Shelley's story is doubled by another irony, for it is his Monster who carries what Victor has lost. The Monster, whose dead body was reanimated through the technological application of the powers of science, is first resurrected into a life of self-awareness through the aesthetic charms of nature. It is the Monster who leads us back to what Victor has sacrificed in the single-minded pursuit of his dream.

The Monster's tale

> I was a poor, helpless, miserable wretch: I knew and could distinguish nothing; but, feeling pain invade me on all sides, I sat down and wept. Soon a gentle light stole over the heavens, and gave me a sensation of pleasure. I started up, and beheld a radiant form rise from among the trees. I gazed with a kind of wonder. It moved slowly, but it enlightened my path.
>
> *(Shelley, 1818)*

Although he still feels confused by the many sounds he hears and the various scents that greet him, the Monster says, "the only object I could distinguish was the bright moon, and I fixed my eyes on that with pleasure."

This attraction to the moon and its light is a counterpart to the lure of the solar light of Victor's Promethean mind.

> Several changes of day and night passed, and the orb of light had greatly lessened when I began to distinguish my sensations from each other. I gradually saw plainly the clear stream that supplied me with drink, and the trees that shaded me with their foliage. I was delighted when I first discovered that a pleasant sound, which often saluted my ears, proceeded from the throats of the little winged animals who had often intercepted the light from my eyes. I began also to observe, with greater accuracy, the forms that surrounded me, and to perceive the boundaries of the radiant roof of light which canopied me.
>
> *(Shelley, 1818)*

This seems no Monster! Indeed, there is hint of a childlike delight in his wonder and his words, as well as a sense of gratitude, and with a feeling of appreciation for these blessings bestowed upon him, he adds, "Sometimes I tried to imitate the pleasant songs of birds, but was unable. Sometimes I wished to express my sensations in my own mode, but the uncouth and inarticulate sounds which broke from me frightened me into silence again" (Shelley, 1818).

But he is not defeated, and, as he continues his story, it becomes quite clear that the bond between his body and nature has been his first education, an education into an aesthetic sensibility, which precedes and even allows his education to continue when he finds Milton's *Paradise Lost*. Before he learns to read that book, we sense in his words that the Monster has been taught by the delights of Nature. He has been educated, as it were, by the book of Nature, drawn into the world through the carnal bond between his body, even in its disfigurement, and the charms of Nature.[8]

"My senses were gratified and refreshed by a thousand scents of delight, and a thousand sights of beauty" (Shelley, 1818). Whereas the solar light of Victor's spectator mind ends in the darkness of death and destruction, the moon's light is what gives birth to the Monster's self-awareness. The product of his creator's utilitarian attitude, the Monster is an emblem of an aesthetic sensibility. His tale describes what Victor Frankenstein comes to realize only too late as he is dying. And yet Victor's sacrifice of an aesthetic sensibility has not only overshadowed the Monster's tale of his aesthetic education, it has also benumbed us even to the necessity for such an education.

Distracted, for example, by the enticements of computer emoticons to express what one feels, or the numbing deadness of our 24/7 news cycles that bombard us with acts of outrageous behavior and political discourtesy not to mention acts of violence, terror and barbaric scenes of cruelty, our capacity to sense the world, to be impregnated by its appeals, to delight in its presence seems increasingly imperiled. In the fraying connection between body and nature, the spectator mind has fled into the digital world. Living on line is fast replacing being in nature, and, as we have described in Question Five, on line our own nature is rapidly being transformed.

But even as we are losing touch with the world of nature, an aesthetic sensibility is in fact so deeply buried in the collective spectator mind that we catch a glimpse of its absence in those benumbing *anesthetic* states of our drug culture with its pharmaceutical cornucopia. There are, for example, antidepressants that promise to take us beyond our states of sadness and opioids to take away our pains both physical and emotional. But this flight from feelings has a price. Opioid use, for example, has become a major health crisis.

But what if our sorrows and our pains are less individual conditions to be treated and more a collective one to be understood?

What if the prophetic expressions of Mary Shelley's story, which appear in the guises of the many crises we face today from the dying of nature as we know it to the god wars and their economic and political consequences, are for the human heart all too much to bear?

In the face of such continuous states of emergency and crisis management, do we seek relief by becoming and remaining anesthetized for as long as possible?

The Monster's tale is a seed of hope to wake up from the anesthetic stupor of the collective spectator mind.

The poetic realism of the world

While Victor Frankenstein is an emblem of the utilitarian attitude of the spectator mind, a mind for no seasons, a mind that has broken the bonds between the sensitive, receptive flesh of the body and the appeals of nature, a mind that has taken leave of its senses, that has become insensible to the charms and delights of the world, the Monster is an emblem of what has been lost, an embodiment of an aesthetic sensibility.[9]

Before we know the natural world in terms of this or that fact, or arrange it in terms of some system of ideas, we are astonished by the sheer "thereness" of nature. Like the Monster was awakened by the moon's light, we are cradled within nature, impregnated as it were by the wind or the trees dancing to its rhythm, inspired by it, taking it in with each breath and, with a slight pause, transforming it on the out breath into a song or perhaps a word, which might exclaim the delight at seeing a tree that is perhaps even more lovely than a poem.[10] Before we make sense of the world we sense it as an appeal that solicits our response. The bird that sings in the morning light turns one's head toward its song.

This bond, this umbilical lifeline as it were, between the sensual flesh of the animate body and the sensuous charms of the natural world, is an aesthetic one. In this erotic dance between body and world, aesthetics is more than a theory of beauty in a philosophy of art criticism. Beauty is, of course, at play in the world's displays, but at its core the word aesthetic means to feel, to sense, to perceive. In this regard, every living creature dwells within its specific aesthetic circle, which can and does overlap across many different species. For example, the look in the eye of a dying seal that has washed ashore on an oil soiled beach can arouse one's sympathy and compassion.

This tie is a primordial bond, an aesthetic sensibility that is the first way of knowing the world and being in it, a coupling between embodied mind and nature, an erotic dance of desire, which discloses the world through and as a mood. In this context, the cycles of one's moody presences mimic the cycles of nature, which dress the world in its changing colors, shadings, temperatures and sounds. Like the natural world, the psychological world has its seasons. This seasonal resonance between psychological life and nature is why it can make perfect sense and even delight one who, when he or she is feeling pulled down into the moody blues, understands this question asked by the poet Pablo Neruda: "Why do leaves commit suicide when they feel yellow?" (1974/1991, p. 5).

But in our disconnect from the natural world, we have, for example, made the ritual of our wintery behaviors, when we might retreat indoors, hunker down with friends and family around the warmth of the house and attend to the falling snow with a quieting of mind, into a psychological pathology: SAD—Seasonal Affective Disorder. The pharmacy beckons with its substances to chase away these "blues."

Desire precedes meaning making! Before mind becomes an interior subject split off from the world as an exterior object, we find ourselves within webs of meanings already made of slender, delicate, diaphanous threads woven in the chiasm of our moods and nature's charms. Before we become a spectator of nature apart from it, we are witnesses in wonder at the world's ordinary miracles. We come to understand the world because we have already been understood by it. In this regard, we might even wonder if all knowing is a coming home.

Beguiled by the world before we have any ambition to explain the world, this primordial ground, which tastes and smells, and touches, and hears, and sees, the world with an almost animal like sensibility, is inevitably forgotten. And yet, it remains a sustaining ground that might return, for example, in moments of loss and grief when all the structures of meaning making have crumbled into dust. When Victor Frankenstein pushes aside his grief at his mother's death, he forsakes this primordial ground of being to create new life in the isolated chambers of his own Promethean mind.

Frankenstein, Elizabeth and the Monster

After the Monster is beguiled by the moon's light, he is drawn to the songs of the birds, and fascinated by their beauty he tries to imitate them. Although he fails, the attempt is a threshold moment when a rhythm is formed between his receptivity to the songs of nature and his response to them. First awakened to himself by the moon's light, he becomes at this threshold a response-able being. In spite of his monstrous appearance, he becomes a person who is able-to-respond to the world when he is addressed by it.

Compared with the Monster, Victor Frankenstein is irresponsible. But this description is not a judgment. On the contrary, it only marks a difference between two sets of values, one that is aesthetic and the other utilitarian. Each value is a way of evaluating the world. While Mary Shelley's story emphasizes the utilitarian values of Victor Frankenstein, the genius of her story is that the Monster carries the pro- phetic warnings about the eclipse of aesthetic values. His outward disfigurement is a visible sign of how this loss of an aesthetic presence to the world disfigures the soul.[11]

In Question Two we saw how Victor Frankenstein describes this contrast in values in terms of how he regards himself in relation to Elizabeth Lavenza. As a man of science, the world, he says, was to him a secret and he was delighted to investigate the facts of the actual world in order to discover them. For Elizabeth Lavenza, on the other hand, the world was a vacancy, which she peopled with her imagination fed by the aerial creations of the poets.

For Victor Frankenstein the contrast in values between himself and the Monster is personified in terms of the scientist and the poet. In this context, Elizabeth Lavenza is strangely twined with the Monster. Both of them are unlike Victor Frankenstein, and both of them pay a price for this difference. Victor dismisses Elizabeth as one whose imaginative wanderings are naïve and childish, and as one whom he says he regards as if she were a beloved pet. Disregarded she eventually becomes the sacrifice to Victor's dream and his work when she is murdered on their wedding night. The Monster, abandoned by his creator, mocked as devil and demon, lives his isolated and miserable existence as an outcast on the margins of the human community.

Twined as they are in this way, Victor's godlike dream shows not only its monstrous face when he creates life apart from the feminine, it also shows the feminine face of the Monster. Indeed, this coupling of Elizabeth and the Monster shows that the Monster as devil and demon has escaped the confines of hell. Mary Shelley's pivotal story as a re-telling of the Christian story of creation, which has dominated western culture for 2000 years, exposes how the demonization of Eve as the spoiler of God's work who brings death into paradise is itself the monstrous act. The worm in the apple, the snake in the garden is the patriarchal god who in Mary Shelley's story has the face of Victor Frankenstein.

What are poets for in a destitute time?

This question comes from the nineteenth century German poet Holderlin's elegy "Bread and Wine." In 1946, after the defeat of Germany and the general ruin that followed in its wake, the philosopher Martin Heidegger said that "we hardly understand the question today" (Heidegger, 1950/1975, p. 91).[12] Yet in his reading of Holderlin's poem, we hear that it is the absence of the gods as an organizing cosmology for human beings that mark destitute times. In their absence we become the measure of all things, and it is within this hollow that Victor Frankenstein does his work. Within this fissure of the human heart, Victor Frankenstein can regard the ground of churchyard cemeteries as devoid of the sacred.

From the trenches of World War I the English poet Wilfred Owen wrote that the duty of the poet is to warn. As this book takes up Mary Shelley's story in its prophetic warnings for our destitute times, it is fitting to quote these words from "The Snow Man" by the poet Wallace Stevens:

> One must have a mind of winter
> To regard the frost and the boughs
> Of the pine-trees crusted with snow
> *(Stevens, 2009, p. 7)*

These three lines so simple in their brevity and so eloquent in their simplicity are created by a poetic mind that contrasts with the spectator mind, the mind that has no seasons. In Stevens's poem the poetic mind is an embodied mind responsive to the winter season of the natural world. It is an aesthetic mind that is impregnated by the pine trees laden with snow, a mind that feels the weight of its chill, a mind, which, in that moment of regarding the frost of the tree, *is* the mind of winter. Or, to personify the point, the poet Wallace Stevens as the mind of winter *is* the Snow Man. He, the poet, knows the winter season not from his room behind a window gazing at a snowman. He knows the winter season more intimately; he knows it by becoming what he knows.[13]

Read this short poem to the end and you might lose your spectator mind. At the very least, you might discover a large crack in the spectator mind that is perhaps made by the Snow Man who has thrown a snowball at you. For the Snow Man is challenging the spectator mind's identification of what is real with what is measured and explained. The Snow Man is saying there is a sense of reality where what is perceived is sifted through imagination. He is re-minding us that empirical realism is a perspective. The Snow Man is calling us back to the poetic realism of the world that is rooted in an embodied aesthetic sensibility. The Snow Man is an avatar of imagination and the specific genius of the poetic mind is that it is vulnerable and permeable to the imagination.

Imagine what is lost if the poetic mind was regarded as SAD, as suffering from a seasonal affective disorder?

A difference would become a diagnosis!

A different way of knowing the world and being in it would be lost!

The poetic realism of the world would be lost in the dubious triumph of empirical realism as the sole measure of what is real and true.

The value and wisdom of the dream

Mary Shelley tells us that Victor Frankenstein and the Monster appeared to her in a waking dream. That admission anticipates by almost a hundred years Freud's 1900 publication of *The Interpretation of Dreams*, which inaugurates psychoanalysis and privileges the dream as the royal road to the unconscious side of mind.

But insofar as it was a waking dream, we could consider Victor Frankenstein and the Monster less as projections emanating from her unconscious mind and more as figures who come to her. As such, we could understand Victor and the Monster as fictional characters, *which*, like stage characters, emotionally touch us with their vital presence. In this context, the dream figures of Victor and his Monster are as real as is the dreamer Mary Shelley, but their reality is more subtle than our identification of reality with our empirical measures. A primary value of the dream, then, is that it radically challenges the hegemony of the awake, conscious mind and opens one to another way of knowing the world and being in it. The dream taken seriously is a way of knowing that is closer to the poetic sensibility described above.[14]

Regardless, however, of whether a dream is treated as a projection of the dreamer's unconscious mind or as an encounter with an autonomous figure, a dream as we discussed in Question Seven faces a dreamer with an ethical challenge and obligation to attend to its presence.

To be present to the dream as an ethical challenge and obligation inverts the usual relationship between the waking mind and the dream. It turns that relationship upside down because it initially suspends the rush of the waking mind to make sense of the dream. In place of that move to interpret the dream and impose that understanding on the dream, the dreamer welcomes the dream with hospitality. This initial act of hospitality is rooted in the very experience of dreaming, for one does not have a dream but is dreamed by the dream. Indeed, from this point of view when a dreamer wakes up and claims the dream by saying "I had a dream," the dreamer is actually falling asleep to the fact that he or she has been dreamed. To be hospitable to the dream, therefore, the dreamer, before milking the dream for its meanings, needs to feed the dream with wonder and step back to cultivate the virtues of slowness, caution, patience and a vulnerable presence. This vulnerable presence is what allows the dreamer to be inspired by the dream, to breathe it in and become impregnated by the dream, sensing it as the way of making sense of it.

Dreamed by the dream, a dreamer can regard its images as nightly guests who knock on the door of the conscious mind. Or perhaps it is more apt to say that insofar as the dream images are uninvited, a dreamer might regard them as strangers who rap rather loudly on the door of the conscious mind.

But what do these nightly guests or uninvited strangers want and what do they bring with them?

However we might regard their presence, they bring news from the margins and with that news an invitation.

Mary Shelley was certainly very familiar with the electrical experiments being done in the late eighteenth century and their claims for re-animating dead tissue. She was quite knowledgeable about these issues and indeed moved in circles with her husband and others where these issues were discussed. That she claimed, therefore, that Victor Frankenstein, the Monster and their story were born in a waking dream is a curious and important detail to be noted.

Her claim not only invites the reader to consider that the dream might have value and wisdom that is other than the reasons of mind, it also invites the reader to read her story as a commentary on the hidden shadows of the Promethean mind. In this context, Mary Shelley's story is the conduit through which Victor Frankenstein and the Monster have become hauntingly living images of the dangers in the collective dream of becoming God.

The Frankenstein Prophecies reads her story in this fashion. It takes up her story not just as her waking dream, but as a dream she was dreaming for us, as a dream of what our future has become.

But this future is not yet a fate to which we are condemned. Reading *Frankenstein; Or, The Modern Prometheus* as a prophetic dream offers a seed of hope if we can attend to the hints she gives to us regarding the value and wisdom of the dream. If we wake up to her waking dream and begin to understand that we are webbed within that dream, then, perhaps, the prophecy becomes an opportunity. The challenge is that it is the Monster who calls, the Monster in exile who is trying to wake us up. However dark he might be, however disturbing his news might be, the dream as a seed of hope lies on the margins of mind.

Victor Frankenstein himself is a harbinger of the difficulty of this challenge. The dream in which he embraces his beloved Elizabeth who turns into the rotting corpse of his dead mother vividly presents the dark, monstrous side of his work. This dream, as the first commentary on his work, is a nightmarish image that addresses him with a radical question regarding the ethics of his wish to be a new creator god. It presents a possibility that he has dismissed in his waking life. But Victor Frankenstein is a deaf man who does not hear the knock on the door, and thus he ignores that possibility. Inhospitable to his dream as he is inhospitable to his Monster in his waking life, the possibility of the dream that he dismisses in daylight returns in that image of the night.

Of course, his refusal is what makes Mary Shelley's story a human tragedy. It holds the tension between the dream as a possibility of change and as a radical challenge that can turn one's life upside down. Even after more than a hundred years of Freud and Jung, we are hardly, if it all, any better at cultivating the dream as a seed of hope.[15] Harvesting that seed takes time and patience, virtues that are quite at odds with our 24/7 light-speed way of life. In addition, regardless of whatever a dream might mean, each dream is a nightly humiliation of the conscious mind, a humbling of its Promethean reach. Every dream is a fall of the disembodied spectator mind into the *humus*, the organic soil of the embodied mind. Brought low in this way, the value and wisdom of the dream is that it can become an education in learning how to listen to what seems and feels radically other. A dream is an education in learning to be receptive as a condition preceding action, a prescription, as it were, for too quick "knee jerk" reactions. Dreaming, we might say, is a kind of continuing education in the night school of the waking mind. Victor Frankenstein seems never to have attended classes.

Have we also been absent?

That absence cautions us not to forget that Mary Shelley's waking dream is still haunting us.[16]

Closing time

Having been in the company of the Monster, lending an ear to his tale told on the margins, I am drawn now to a memory of a time spent in a wilderness preserve in South Africa. It seems an appropriate way to bring this narrative to a close, for, as I look back on that experience, it was a moment where, without knowing it, *The Frankenstein Prophecies* was being incubated.

The leopard and the moon

Before I became part of an on line dream group on climate change, I had a vivid dream while in the Umfolzi preserve in South Africa. Insofar as dreams are more than personal and tap into cultural, historical and ecological levels of the dreaming mind, this dream of a leopard seems to be a commentary on how the Promethean dream of science and technology has broken the relationship between our instinctual body and the body of nature.[17]

The animating spirit of nature has been exiled and the leopard in this dream is an emblem of the Monster addressing us from the margins.

It was already late evening when we gathered to wait and watch for the leopard's return. Earlier that day, we had found the remains of a partially eaten bushbuck. Surprisingly the leopard had not protected it from scavengers, and we had spent some time positioning the kill in a tree. As we did so a few drops of its blood seeped onto our clothes binding the leopard and us together.

Framed by the branches and leaves of the tree where we had placed the buck, the moon was larger and closer to the earth than I had ever seen, its yellow light casting shadows over the small circle of our vigil. Beyond its light the bush receded into an endless blackness. In moonlight we waited in the night silence for the return of the leopard. At some point during our vigil, I slipped into a state of reverie, or was it a dream?

When night came our ancestors would have gathered in the darkness drawn together by their fear. The leopard would have been out there as they waited for the morning sun. But for a few the moon's yellow light might have overcome their fear, and for a moment they might have been entranced and wondered about its radiant mystery.

"Hello Houston. Tranquility Base here. The Eagle has landed."

The words awakened me from my reverie, or was it a dream? The night had grown colder and Michael, our guide seemed to be asleep. Our tracker, Joe, perched atop our jeep was as motionless as a statue. The silence of the bush was broken only occasionally by the soft body of the wind gliding through the darkness. The moon that had been so near was now far away.

We had waited but the leopard never came. We were too far away, and yet I knew the leopard had been there that night and through long and countless nights, watching us and waiting for us to return to remind us of who we are and what we have forgotten.

The primary focus of the on line group on climate change has been on the dream and two types of animal dreams have stood out for me. First, there are those dreams in which animals are in peril and seem to be making an appeal for us to recognize our responsibilities toward them. Second, there are some very striking dreams in which the animal is no longer simply waiting for us to return, but is pulling us into the maelstroms of climate change.

How might we respond to such dreams especially if the value and wisdom of the dream is that it offers the dreamer another possible perspective to view the issue of climate change, to attend to the perspective of the animals coming forth out of their exile on the margins?

Are we being summoned by them to sense the issue of climate change as they experience it?

Are they asking us to let go of the fixed assumption that we are dreaming of animals and consider that they are dreaming us? The poet Rilke is quite at home with such a question. In the *Duino Elegies* he says:

> and already the knowing brutes are aware
> that we don't feel very securely at home
> within our interpreted world.
> *(Rilke, 1939, p. 21)*

Per Espen Stoknes's recent book has the provocative title, *What We Think About When We Try Not to Think About Global Warming* (2015). His book is important and insightful, but apart from a very few cursory mentions of Jung and Freud, there is no real consideration of how unconscious dynamics have played a fundamental role in the creation of climate crises, and therefore how their absence impacts the ways we react to the crises. Indeed, if we riff off the title of his book, then we must say that the neglect of the dream and its wisdom is one of the things we try not to think about when we do think about global warming. *The Frankenstein Prophecies* shows the necessity to take up Victor Frankenstein's story and the Monster's untold tale as a collective cultural dream that we are still dreaming today. Attending to how dreams offer us another perspective about climate change might even be necessary for our survival.

Notes

1 Mary Shelley's story was written in three parts, which in the 1818 edition are presented as three volumes. The words of Milton appear on the title page of each of the three volumes, which emphasize that Mary Shelley has designed the story of Victor Frankenstein and his Monster in terms of the biblical tale of the fall from paradise. In this context, her story is a cautionary tale of the dangers of the scientific and technological powers Victor Frankenstein uses to become a new creator god. His Monster is an emblem of Adam and a prophetic embodiment of who we are today as we continue Frankenstein's dream to create life and resurrect the dead. It is a dream that has become our nightmare. In essence this is the fundamental theme and the motivating force of *The Frankenstein Prophecies*.

2 In 1822 Percy Bysshe Shelley drowned after his boat, *Don Juan*, was overturned in a storm. Ten days later when his body was found it was cremated. His heart, however, which was badly calcified because of his early bouts with tuberculosis, would not burn. Although his friend, Leigh Hunt, initially kept it, Percy's heart was eventually given to Mary Shelley, who did not bury it with his remains in a cemetery in Rome. A year after she died in 1851 his heart was found in her desk. In 1889 after their son, Percy Florence Shelley, died, the poet's heart was laid to rest in the family tomb.

3 For an excellent presentation of these shadows of love, see Veronica Goodchild, *Eros and Chaos: The Sacred Mysteries and Dark Shadows of Love* (2001). Regarding my claim that Mary Shelley's story is a love story when the Monster's tale is given a place, Guillermo del Toro said in his Academy Award speech for *The Shape of Water* that his film is a love story. He added, "Love is stronger than hatred and it is much more powerful than fear. Love is the antidote to what we are living today." For details about his film see note two in the Introduction.

4 I use the term mankind and not human kind not just to stay within the cultural and historical context of his time, but also to stay in touch with Victor Frankenstein's patriarchal attitude, which is clearly indicated in his description of Elizabeth Lavenza quoted in Question Two.

5 In Franz Kafka's shockingly disturbing story, *The Metamorphosis*, Gregor Samsa's transformation into a gigantic insect illustrates his mind numbing existence as a cipher in a bureaucratic machine. Published in 1915 is Gregor Samsa kin of Victor Frankenstein's "Monster," his Monster updated as it were to fit the times, a kind of robotic life, like the robotic voice at the end of a telephone, which in its mimicry of a human voice is programed to be unresponsive to anything but its program?

   Hello! Is anybody out there?

   Kafka's nightmare, the soulless bureaucrat whose behavior is scheduled by utilitarian values like efficiency, becomes even more disturbing in the figure of Adolf Eichmann. Eichmann personifies the banality of evil, which is the phrase that Hannah Arendt used in the subtitle of her book, *Eichmann in Jerusalem* published in 1963. For Eichmann, who was charged with the arrangements that had to be made to transport Jews to the death camps, the only questions were how efficiently and quickly it could be done and the calculations that were necessary to do so at the lowest cost to the German war effort.

The trains had to run on time and to maximize their use every inch of space in them was to be utilized. Who was in those trains was not part of the equation. What mattered was the job Eichmann was supposed to do. In this context, the countless number of human beings on their way to the death camps were simply cargo. The trains were in all respects freight trains.

When Eichmann was on trial in Jerusalem he stood behind a glass enclosure ostensibly to protect him. Regardless of the reason, however, the place where he stood to give his defense displays the moral position of the man and his work. It stands as an image of the spectator mind behind the window, separated and cut off from any moral attachment to others. Behind his window, Eichmann was incapable of any moral sympathy.

Hannah Arendt's book created a storm of controversy because she courageously dared to suggest a question: Who is the monster? In this regard, the glass enclosure was more than a window. It was also a mirror. Eichmann was not being excused for his crimes, but he was not to be made into the convenient scapegoat, which would free each of us from looking in the mirror.

6 As we saw in Question Five, Ray Kurzweil is a prime example of someone who believes he has succeeded.

7 I quoted this passage in Question Six to illustrate how Victor Frankenstein's Promethean dream has become a prophecy of the dying of nature and has made each of us homeless in the wired webbed world. In this question, this passage illustrates Victor Frankenstein's utilitarian attitude toward Nature.

8 For Galileo the book of nature is written in mathematical symbols and it us who are meant to read that book. The contrast with the Monster's being educated by the book of Nature is the contrast between Victor Frankenstein, a dramatic emblem of the spectator mind behind the window, who takes the measure of Nature and the Monster who, dwelling within Nature, is enchanted by its charms.

One other point to make here is that this contrast between two different ways of being in the world is also a contrast between two different ways of speaking about it. One way uses the active voice of the verb in which one is the doer of the action, the one who reads the book. The other way uses the passive voice of the verb in which one is the recipient of an action, the one who is read by the book.

This contrast is part of the cultural history of the scientific-technological attitude. For the spectator mind the passive voice is very much identified with passivity and its negative connotations. This attitude loses the sense of the passive voice as receptivity. Indeed, the receptive nature of our being is ultimately identified with the condition of being a body, which acts as a drag on the Promethean leaps of the disembodied spectator mind. This cultural history is even built into our computers, which generally prompt us to change passive to active voice. No time to be receptively passive when at the computer terminal information moves almost at the speed of light.

9 *Technology as Symptom and Dream* (Romanyshyn, 1989/2006) which details the creation of the modern scientific-technological world-view, is the scholarly text, which in this book is being retold in the context of Mary Shelley's dramatic story. See note eight above and notes three and five in Question One for details about the spectator mind.

10 The allusion, of course, is to the poem "Trees" written in 1913 by Joyce Kilmer.

11 I am using the term soul in the psychological sense described in the work of James Hillman. See especially his groundbreaking book, *Re-Visioning Psychology* (1975).

12 POETRY, LANGUAGE, THOUGHT by MARTIN HEIDEGGER. Translations and Introduction by Albert Hofstadter. Copyright (c) 1971 by Martin Heidegger. Courtesy of HarperCollins Publishers.

13 Is he serious? Am I being serious? Yes, he is and so am I. It gets cold if you linger in winter with the Snow Man, but the Snow Man is not yet done with us. He is something of a trickster. Sifted through the poet's imagination, was he created by Wallace Stevens? Is Wallace Stevens the god who made him, like Victor Frankenstein made his

Monster? Or, is the trickster Snow Man with his mind of winter suggesting that he made himself through the poet?

Who writes the Poem?

Is it Wallace Stevens writing about the Snow Man?

Is the Snow Man writing himself through Wallace Stevens?

The poetic realism of the world is not fixed. It is a fluid realism in which the back and forth flow of Wallace Stevens and the Snow Man confuses the question of authorship. In this chiasm, then, Wallace Stevens *is* and *is not* the Snow Man, and the Snow Man *is* and *is not* the poet.

But we should not conclude this reflection without this serious question: Is there a Snow Woman?

14 Victor Frankenstein is born from Mary Shelley's waking dream, and the Monster is born of Victor Frankenstein's dream. We are still dreaming these dreams as our nightmare whose themes show themselves as the prophetic crises explored in this book. See Question Seven, note six and Question One, note nine. As a seed of hope in her story, the wisdom of the dream is that it offers us a way of approaching these crises in terms of the values of a poetic sensibility rooted in the post Enlightenment Romantic tradition that affirms dream, night, the animated spirit of nature and the reality of imagination.

15 See James Hillman and Michael Ventura *We've Had a Hundred Years of Psychotherapy and the World Is Getting Worse*(1993).

See also my two essays "Phenomenology as a Poetic Realism," and "Conversations in the Gap Between Mind and Soul." Both essays, which are available as PDF files on my website http://robertromanyshyn.jigsy.com/, describe an approach to working with dreams as a possibility of possibility. This approach attends to the imperative mood of the dream world and takes up its images and stories as possibilities to be rehearsed, tried on, as it were. In this regard, this approach to dream work lingers for a while in reverie, in the place between the night and the day worlds. Between dreaming and being fully awake, this approach does not rush into interpreting the dream's meanings. Rather, it cultivates a change of mood toward the subjunctive mood of what might be, a move into the images as what are perhaps possibilities to be embodied. Working with dreams in this fashion, I have found that it helps one to see the day world in different ways, often loosening up fixed and rigid ways of being. The subjunctive mood of dream work colors the day world in a different way. It is, as it were, a new prescription for the eyes of the soul.

16 Working on this book, I have had numerous experiences of being worked over by it not the least of which has been how my dreams have challenged me. One dream, for example, takes place in a huge auditorium where I am unexpectedly asked to give a talk about dreams. The auditorium is filled with hundreds of people and I have no lectern from which to speak and no microphone to address such a large audience. As I begin my remarks by saying a dream is a nightly humiliation of the waking mind, the crowd becomes very distracted and distracting. They are not able to hear me not simply because of the absence of any microphone, but also and more pointedly in terms of the content of the remarks.

The dream as a marginal experience for the waking mind poses a difficult challenge.

Is the dream saying that the challenges that it imposes are not easily heard by the collective waking mind?

And, perhaps, is it also addressing me with this question: Is this whole project a quixotic quest?

17 In *The Wounded Researcher: Research with Soul in Mind* (2007), I describe these four levels of the unconscious mind and apply them to the research process. The central claim in that book is that the scientific idea of objectivity as the absence of the researcher from the research process conceals not only a researcher's biases, but also his or her unconscious complex relation to the work. The idea of a neutral observer is a myth of the scientific paradigm. We approach objectivity through deep subjectivity.

REFERENCES

Arasse, D. (1991). *The Guillotine and the Terror* (Christopher Miller, Trans.). Harmondsworth: Penguin.

Arendt, H. (1963). *Eichmann in Jerusalem: A Report on the Banality of Evil*. New York: Viking Press.

Arnold, M. (1867/2012). *Dover Beach and other Poems*. Mineola, NY: Dover Books.

Atienza, B., Horwits, M., and King, J. (Producers), and Bayona, J. A. (Director). (2016). *A Monster Calls*. United States, Universal Pictures.

Bright, B. (2012). Leaving Home, Losing Home: A Social and Symbolic Look at Migration. Towards Beginnings: Images of End, special issue edited by Roxanne Partridge and Gustavo Beck. *The Journal of Archetypal Studies* 2, pp. 191–211.

Bright, B. (2015). Borders and Belonging: Archetypal and Ecological Aspects of "Home" in Homer's Odyssey. *Quadrant* 45 (1), pp. 33–47.

Bruch, H. (1979). *The Golden Cage: The Enigma of Anorexia Nervosa*. New York: Vintage.

Bukatman, S. (1993). *Terminal Identity: The Virtual Subject in Post Modern Science Fiction*. Durham, NC: Duke University Press.

Burnside, J. (2017). The Real Value of Space Travel is Recognising the Beauty of our Planet. *New Statesman*, July 7–13.

Cioran, E. (1973). *The Trouble with Being Born* (R. Howard, Trans). New York: Arcade Publishing.

Cohn, N. (1977). *Europe's Inner Demons*. New York: New American Library.

Corbett, L. (2018). *Understanding Evil: A Psychotherapist's Guide*. London: Routledge.

cummings, e. e. (1926/1959). *100 poems*. New York: Grove Weidenfeld.

Dale, J. (Producer), and del Toro, G. (Director). (2017). *The Shape of Water*. United States, Fox Searchlight Studios.

Descartes, R. (1637/1971). The Dioptrics, in *Descartes: Philosophical Writings* (E. Anscombe, Ed. and P. T. Geach, Trans.) Indianapolis, IN: Bobbs-Merril.

Donne, J. (1941). *The Complete Poetry and Selected Prose of John Donne and the Complete Poetry of William Blake*. New York: The Modern Library.

Dormehi, L. (2017). *Thinking Machines: The Quest for Artificial Intelligence and Where It's Taking Us Next*. New York: Tarcher Perigree.

Dowd, M. (September 23, 2017). Will Mark Zuckerberg "Like" This Column? Sunday Review Section, *New York Times*. p. 9.

Eliot, T. S. (1934). *T. S. Eliot The Waste Land and other Poems*. New York: Harcourt, Brace & World.

Forster, E. M. (1980). *Aspects of the Novel*. New York: Penguin Books.

Freidman, T. L. (January 11, 2017). Online and Scared. *The New York Times*, Op-Ed, p. A23.

Freud, S. (1930). Civilization and Its Discontents, in *The Standard Edition of the Complete Psychological Works of Sigmund Freud* (James Strachey, Trans). Vol. 21. London: Hogarth Press.

Goodchild, V. (2001). *Eros and Chaos: The Sacred Mysteries and Dark Shadows of Love*. Lake Worth, FL: Nicolas-Hays.

Harari, Y. N. (2011). *Sapiens: A Brief History of Humankind*. London: Vintage Books.

Harari, Y. N. (2017). *Homo Deus: A Brief History of Tomorrow*. New York: Harper Collins.

Heidegger, M. (1969). *Discourse on Thinking*. New York: Harper Torchbooks.

Heidegger, M. (1950/1975). What are Poets for?, in *Poetry, Language, Thought* (Albert Hofstadter, Trans.) New York: Harper Colophon Books.

Heidegger, M. (1955/1977). *The Question Concerning Technology* (William Lovitt, Trans.). New York: Harper Colophon Books. Hillman, J. (1975). *Re-Visioning Psychology*. New York: Harper Perennial.

Hillman, J. (1989). *The Dream and the Underworld*. New York: Harper and Row.

Hillman, J., and Ventura, M. (1993). *We've Had a Hundred Years of Psychotherapy and the World is Getting Worse*. San Francisco, CA: Harper Collins.

Hitchcock, S. T. (2007). *Frankenstein: A Cultural History*. New York: W. W. Norton & Company.

Illich, I. (1970). *Deschooling Society*. New York: Harper & Row.

Janus Head. (2008). Special Issue: J. H. van den Berg, 10 (2). Amherst, NY: Trivium Publications.

Jung, C. G. (1946/1960). On the Nature of the Psyche, in *The Structure and Dynamics of the Psyche* (R. F. C. Hull, Trans.). In *The Collected Works of C. G. Jung* (H. Read et al., Series Eds.), Vol. 8. Princeton, NJ: Princeton University Press.

Jung, C. G. (1965). *Memories, Dreams, Reflections*. New York: Vintage Books.

Jung, C. G. (1957/1967) Commentary on the Secret of the Golden Flower (R. F. C. Hull, Trans.), in *Alchemical Studies, The Collected Works of C. G. Jung* (H. Read et al., Series Eds.), Vol. 13, para. 54. Princeton, NJ: Princeton University Press.

Jung, C. G. (1958/1973). Answer to Job. *Fiftieth Anniversary Edition, C. G. Jung* (R. F. C. Hull, Trans.). Princeton, NJ: Princeton University Press. Kaufmann, W. (1959). *The Portable Nietzsche*. Selected and Translated with an Introduction, Preface, and Notes. New York: Viking Penguin.

Kilmer, J. (1913/2018). *Trees and other Poems*. Classic Reprint Series. Retrieved from www.forgottenbooks.com.

Klein, N. (2014). *This Changes Everything*. New York: Simon & Schuster.

Kurzweil, R. (1999). *The Age of Spiritual Machines*. New York: Penguin Books.

Kurzweil, R. (2005). *The Singularity Is Near: When Humans Transcend Biology*. New York: Penguin Books.

Lanier, Jaron (2010). *You Are Not a Gadget: A Manifesto*. New York: Vintage Books.

Mansouri, F. (2010). *Longing for Belonging: Exile and Homecoming in Rumi's Poetry and Jung's Psychology*. PhD Thesis, Pacifica Graduate Institute.

Merchant, C. (1983). *The Death of Nature: Women, Ecology and the Scientific Revolution*. New York: Harper & Row.

Merleau-Ponty, M. (1942/1963). *The Structure of Behavior* (Alden L. Fisher, Trans.). Boston, MA: Beacon Press.

Merleau-Ponty, M. (1945/1962). *Phenomenology of Perception* (Colin Smith, Trans). London: Routledge & Kegan Paul. Merleau-Ponty, M. (1968). *The Visible and the Invisible* (Alphonso Lingis, Trans.). Evanston, IL: Northwestern University Press.

Mugerauer, R. (2008). *Heidegger and Homecoming: The Leitmotif in the Later Writings.* Toronto: University of Toronto Press.

Neruda, P. (1974/1991). *The Book of Questions* (William O'Day, Trans). Port Townsend, WA: Copper Canyon Press.

Neumann, E. (1973). *Depth Psychology and a New Ethic.* New York: Harper Torchbooks. Oates, J. C. (1984). Frankenstein's Fallen Angel, in Mary Shelley, *Frankenstein; Or, the Modern Prometheus.* Berkeley: University of California Press.

O'Connell, M. (2017). *To Be a Machine: Adventures Among Cyborgs, Utopians, Hackers, and the Futurists Solving the Modest Problem of Death.* New York: Doubleday.

Oldenburg, R. (1989/1999). *The Great Good Place.* Cambridge, MA: Da Capo Press.

Piore, A. (2017). *The Body Builders: Inside the Science of the Engineered Human.* New York: Ecco/Harper Collins.

Ragain, K. V. (2006). *Archetypal Threads in the Experience of Being Adopted.* Unpublished doctoral dissertation. Pacifica Graduate Institute, Carpinteria, CA.

Ricoeur, P. (1970). *Freud and Philosophy: An Essay on Interpretation* (Dennis Savage, Trans.). New Haven, CT: Yale University Press.

Rilke, R. M. (1934). *Letters to a Young Poet* (M. D. Herter Norton, Trans.). New York: W. W. Norton & Company.

Rilke, R. M. (1939). *Duino Elegies* (J. B. Leishman and Stephen Spender, Trans.). New York: W. W. Norton & Company.

Rochman, B. (2017). *How Genetic Technologies Are Changing the Way We Have Kids.* New York: Sci Am/ Farrar, Strauss & Giroux.

Rojcewicz, R. (2006). *The Gods and Technology: A Reading of Heidegger.* Albany: State University of New York Press. Romanyshyn, R. D. (1992). The Body as Historical Matter and Cultural Symptom, in *Giving the Body Its Due: Challenges to a Cartesian Metaphysics*, Maxine Sheets-Johnstone (Editor). Albany: State University of New York Press.

Romanyshyn, R. D. (1999). *The Soul in Grief: Love, Death and Transformation*: Berkeley, CA: North Atlantic Press.

Romanyshyn, R. (2001). *Mirror and Metaphor: Images and Stories of Psychological Life.* Pittsburgh, PA: Trivium Publications.

Romanyshyn, R. (2002). *Ways of the Heart: Essays Toward an Imaginal Psychology.* Pittsburgh, PA: Trivium Publications.

Romanyshyn, R. D. (1989/2006). *Technology as Symptom and Dream.* London: Routledge.

Romanyshyn, R. (2007). *The Wounded Researcher: Research with Soul in Mind.* New Orleans, LA: Spring Journal Books.

Romanyshyn, R. (2011). The Body in Psychotherapy: Contributions of Merleau-Ponty, in *Body, Mind and Healing After Jung: A Space of Questions*, Raya Jones (Editor). London: Routledge.

Romanyshyn, R. (2016). Terminal Talk: Reflections on Thinking and Saying in the Digital World, in *Depth Psychology and The Digital Age*, Bonnie Bright (Editor). Depth Insights.

Rowland, S. (2005). *Jung as a Writer.* London: Routledge.

Scofield, T., Tanner, D.Morehead, C.Till, L., and Doedger, F. (Producers). (2015). *The Frankenstein Chronicles* (Series). United States, Rainmark Films.

Shakespeare, W. (1623/2000). *The Tempest.* New York: Penguin Classics.

Sheehan, T. (2015). *Making Sense of Heidegger: A Paradigm Shift*. London: Rowman and Littlefield.

Shelley, M. (1818). *Frankenstein; Or, the Modern Prometheus*. Project Gutenberg. Retrieved from www.gutenberg.org/files/84/84-h/84-h.htm

Sipiora, M. (1991). Heidegger and Epideictic Discourse: The Rhetorical Performance of Meditative Thinking, *Philosophy Today* 35 (3), pp. 239–253.

Slater, G. (1997). Re-Sink the Titanic. *Spring, A Journal of Archetype and Culture* 62, pp. 104–120.

Slater, G. (2006). Cyborgian Drift: Resistance Is Not Futile. *Spring, A Journal of Archetype and Culture* 75, pp. 171–195.

Stevens, W. (2009). The Snow Man, in *Wallace Stevens Selected Poems* (John N. Serio, Ed.). New York: Alfred A. Knopf.

Stoknes, P. E. (2015). *What We Think About When We Try Not To Think About Global Warming*. White River Junction, VT: Chelsea Green Publishing.

Turkle, S. (2011). *Alone Together: Why We Expect More from Technology and Less from Each Other*. New York: Basic Books.

Turkle, S. (September 27, 2015). Stop Googling. Let's Talk. *The New York Times*, Sunday Review.

Van den Berg, J. H. (1966). *The Psychology of the Sickbed*. Pittsburgh, PA: Duquesne University Press.

Wertheim, M. (1999). *The Pearly Gates of Cyberspace*. New York: W. W. Norton & Company.

Wiezenbaum, J. (1976). *Computer Power and Human Reason: From Judgment to Calculation*. New York: W. H. Freeman.

Yeats, W. B. (1919/1956). *The Collected Poems of William Butler Yeats*. New York: Macmillian.

Yonck, R. (2017). *Heart of the Machine: Our Future in a World of Artificial Intelligence*. New York: Arcade Publishing.

INDEX